MINI-MESSAGES FOR
Maximum Living

Printed in the United States of America.
ISBN# 978-0-9801644-3-5

Written by Sidney Fontenot
Compiled by Debbie Fontenot McCormick
www.teamedupconsulting.com

MINI-MESSAGES FOR
Maximum Living

A COLLECTION OF INSPIRATIONAL
MESSAGES FOR LIVING A LIFE
OF SUCCESS AND SIGNIFICANCE.

SIDNEY FONTENOT

Endorsements

"I have known Rev. Sidney Fontenot for thirty nine years and it is an honor for me to set a seal of endorsement upon both this man and his writings. He has served me as both a mentor and spiritual father, in our Christian journey. Brother Sidney is a gifted writer and most impressive is his God-breathed ability and his innateness to say so MUCH in so little space! His "mini-messages" speak volumes to Christians across the entire Body of Christ, the whole gamut of Christianity! I have always admired Sidney's grace in being able to speak with moral clarity in a "denomination-less" expression! Without any reservation, I recommend both this author and his creative messages!"
Richard A. Baggett, Th.D, M.Div
Author, More Than Survivors

"Pastor Fontenot's words are like precious gems that have been skillfully cut and polished. Maybe someone else said or thought the same words, but once they came as finished product from Sidney, their meaning and value had clarity and brilliance as never before. They are everyone unique and insightful. Pastor Fontenot's words of personal care and his sermons across his pulpit, that were spoken to me as a young boy, have lasted me a lifetime. As a pastor in need of inspiration, I constantly anticipate my e-mail message from Partners in Missions, as the words of my divinely appointed shepherd pastor ever helps me find the green pastures and still waters of life! I rest assured that the memorializing of Sidney's mini-messages in a book will bless thousands of others as they have and will continue to inspire mine."
Louis Green
Senior Pastor, Turning Point Worship Center

"Sidney Fontenot's mini-messages apply to all phases of life and are where Christianity hits the pavement in that they are not only deeply spiritual but refreshingly practical. Like appetizers before a meal, these mini-messages are morsels of inspiration for the soul that leave you wanting more."

Dr. Ronnie Burke
Pastor, Maplewood First Baptist Church

"Sidney Fontenot explains in simple, power-packed words the Good News about how the birth, death, and resurrection of Jesus Christ has broken the bondage of sin and opened the doors to God's kingdom by healing the broken heart of one individual at a time so that the glory of God can fill the whole earth. These mini-messages focus on individual and corporate living experiences to demonstrate how God has provided all that we need for maximum living."

Jerry Micelle, Ph.D.

"I am pleased and honored to write this endorsement for my friend and mentor, Reverend Sidney Fontenot. I have known Bro. Sidney to be a devoted husband, father and pastor. His insight, calm demeanor, faithfulness and care for his fellow man are never more evident than in his mini-messages. My desire for this book is that the Jesus experienced and written about by Bro. Sidney will become a reality in your life as He has in mine."

Eudice E. Fontenot, M.D.,
Pediatric Cardiologist

"It has been a pleasure to have assisted Sidney Fontenot in publishing his mini-messages in our newspaper, *American Press*. On many, many occasions, I feel that his messages were written JUST FOR ME! He has been a great inspiration in my life and a very positive role model. If I could just have a little bit of the wisdom God has placed in his heart, I would consider myself blessed."

Karen Cole,
American Press

Dedication

No one does anything worthwhile without others' contributions.

This book is dedicated to my Mom, Delores Christine Fontenot, who tirelessly and enthusiastically served as "chief editor and encourager" for Dad as he developed these weekly mini-messages throughout the years. You have always been, and through the printing of this book will continue to be, a ministering team.

Along with Mom, countless friends have prayed for and financially supported this ministry through Partners In Missions. Our entire family gratefully acknowledges and sincerely thanks each of you, "For we are laborers together with God" (1 Corinthians 3:9).

A Note About

THE MINI-MESSAGES

The pages of this book capture over 200 of my favorite mini-messages written by my dad, Reverend Sidney Fontenot. Very early in his ministry, Dad distinguished himself in our community as a pastor, evangelist, and missionary who reaches people where they are; convinced those who most need to hear the message of salvation would likely hear it least. My brothers and I saw in him a model of how Jesus ministered—going to the people rather than waiting for the people to come to him. One of the most practical ways he did this was by buying ad space and publishing a weekly series of mini-messages—concise, powerful, faith-based messages around practical day-to-day life issues we all face—messages with a catchy title that people who may never enter the doors of a church would want to read.

The first mini-message was published more than twenty-five years ago in the Lake Charles *American Press* as well as in other local newspapers that serve our five-parish region of Southwest Louisiana and are now also distributed through an e-mail ministry and aired weekly on the radio. Dad's wisdom-filled words, whether spoken or written, have always challenged me to live set-apart from the influence of popular culture and to live set-upon the Word of God. I trust they will do the same for you!

A Note About
THE AUTHOR

Growing up in the presence and under the influence of such a wise, generous, godly man—a man I have the distinct privilege of calling Dad—has made all the difference in my life. My Dad was born during the Great Depression and grew up as the younger of two brothers of hard working, French-speaking parents in a farming community in southwest Louisiana. In fact, he didn't learn his first words of English until he entered the first grade. Dad went on to graduate from Bible College with a bachelor's degree in Theology, became an ordained minister, and traveled in Central and South American and extensively in the Caribbean on mission trips. Most of the time, he did all this while juggling the demands of farming to make ends meet.

Dad has an unquenchable love for life, for learning, for words. He can often be found in his favorite chair surrounded by books and note pads and scraps of paper . . . reading, contemplating, writing. Just by way of his daily example, he instilled in me the importance of being a lifelong learner rather than being limited by "formal" years of education.

He is a gifted communicator and a devoted husband and father who loves and serves people as Christ loved and served. Of all the characteristics I deeply admire in Dad, chief among them is that he is exactly the same person in private as he is in public—faithful, loving, sincere, respectful, kind, God-honoring. He is authentic—the real deal—a man of unwavering character! He set the tone in our home of what it looks like to abide in Christ all day, every day. As a result, his life reflects a life well lived.

A Note to Dad

Proverbs 20:7 says, "The just man walketh in his integrity; his children are blessed after him." Because of your faithful walk with God and your integrity in living life, you have established a rich, inspiring legacy for generations to come. What a gift you have given us—your children, grandchildren and future generations—a gift no amount of inheritance could ever buy. You don't tell us how to live; you simply live and let us watch you do it. We have seen up close what a life of success and significance really looks like and we are blessed indeed to call you Dad! You are cherished, respected, admired, and deeply loved by all who know you—most of all by your family. You are a shining beacon of light in a dull, dark world! May God continue to use your gift of words to touch our hearts and challenge our minds for many, many years to come.

Your baby girl, always!

Deb

Table of Contents

Life's Supreme Purpose 1

You Are Free To Succeed 2

He Who Has Ears to Hear 3

Practicing the Sacrament of Living 4

Triage (Sort or Choose) 5

Are You a Giver, a Getter, or Both .6

Choose the Right Side, Always 7

All a Little Bit Crazy 8

Congratulations to All the Grads .9

Dog—Gone Happy 10

Freedom Is a Door for Good or Evil 11

Give Dad a Feeling 12

Give Thanks with a Grateful Heart 13

Let's Join the Witness Team, Today 14

Our Christian Power Source 15

Patience Is a Necessary Life Ingredient 16

The Deep Calls unto the Deep 17

The Golden Rule Contemplated 18

The Ordinary Things of Life 19

The Sword of the Lord and of Gideon 20

The Great Imperative 21

The Gospel, Contemplated 22

Two Moms Sharing One Heart 23

We Are All Called To Saintly Living 24

We Are All Invited To Walk With God 25

WE ARE THE BODY OF CHRIST 26

ATHENS 2004: GOLD, SMILES, AND TEARS 27

CHRISTMAS IS ABOUT A FATHER'S SEARCH 28

DRIVEN BY LOVE 29

GOOD NEWS FROM THE GRAVEYARD 30

IN YOUR PATIENCE POSSESS YE YOUR SOULS 31

LORD TEACH US TO PRAY 32

OPEN THE DOOR—DUMMY! 33

THE BIBLE CALL IS A "HURRY UP" CALL 34

THERE IS NO LOSS 35

THE BIBLE SPEAKS TO THE WEAK, THE POOR, THE FEW 36

THE CHRISTIAN REMEDY IS WITHIN 37

THE GREATEST GIFT EVER GIVEN 38

THE POWER AND EFFECT OF DEEP FEELINGS 39

THERE IS GOOD NEWS FROM THE CROSS 40

THEY NEED NOT DEPART 41

WAS IT CHRISTMAS OR XMAS? 42

WHO IS JESUS—WHY DID HE COME? 43

YOU HAVE NOT PASSED THIS WAY BEFORE 44

YOU MUST LIKE YOURSELF 45

JESUS KNOWS 46

I KNOW SOMETHING GOD HAS FORGOTTEN 47

I CALLED MY FRIEND: "THE BODY" 48

HOW TO AVOID A DAMAGED FAITH 49

HOSTAGE TO OUR HANG-UPS 50

HAPPY FATHER'S DAY, DADS 51

GOD'S GRACE 52

A PRIVATE OR A SHARED FAITH 53

NAME DROPPING 54

A JOURNEY OF CHANGE 55

A SILENT MESSAGE ON A BUSY DAY 56

A SOCIETY WITH PREDATORS 57

ALL KNEE-MAIL WILL BE ANSWERED 58

ACCENTUATE THE POSITIVE 59

APPLYING GOOD MAINTENANCE TO RELIGIOUS LIFE 60

CALLED TO INCONVENIENCE 61

CONTINUING IN COMMITMENT 62

DECLARATION OF DEPENDENCE ON GOD 63

FRIENDLY FIRE 64

GOD'S LAWS ARE GOOD, REASONABLE AND JUST 65

MAN'S LAST REFUGE FROM GOD 66

MIRACLES ARE FEW 67

MEMORIAL DAY IS SACRED 68

LET US PAY UP OUR "THANK YOU DEBT" AND STAY CURRENT . .69

LET US CELEBRATE OUR LABOR WITH JOY 70

I OWE YOU A DEBT AND I MUST PAY IT 71

GOD BLESS AMERICA—LAND THAT WE LOVE 72

FORGIVE QUICKLY AND FORGET PROMPTLY 73

FOOL, FOOLS AND FOOLS FOR CHRIST 74

BE FAIR, HONEST AND RESPECTFUL 75

A WELL PLANNED CHRISTMAS 76

A GOOD TIME FOR AN ATTITUDE ADJUSTMENT 77

WE ARE SOCIAL CREATURES 78

THY KINGDOM COME 79

THERE IS A GOOD KIND OF ADDICTION 80

THERE ARE TWO OPTIONS ONLY 81

THE POWER OF WORDS 82

THE LOVE OF MONEY IS THE ROOT OF ALL EVIL 83

THE LOST COIN 84

THE HIGHEST CREDENTIAL ON EARTH 85

THE FIRST QUESTION, THE FIRST ANSWER 86

THE ART OF BELONGING 87

ROMANS CHAPTER 8—THE MISSING CHAPTER 88

POWER AND RESTRAINT 89

MOTHERHOOD IS AMAZING IN ALL SPECIES OF LIFE 90

THE OLD RUGGED CROSS 91

THE DAY OF SMALL THINGS 92

PROCRASTINATION (THE ART OF PUTTING OFF) 93

OVERFLOWING ABUNDANCE 94

OUR SECURITY—ITS LIMITS 95

NEW TIME RELIGION 96

THE REVIVAL WE NEED (1 OF 4) 97

THE REVIVAL WE NEED (2 OF 4) 98

THE REVIVAL WE NEED (3 OF 4) 99

THE REVIVAL WE NEED (4 OF 4) .100

THE ULTIMATE POVERTY—THE ULTIMATE WEALTH 101

TRUE RELIGION IS ALL ABOUT A CONNECTION 102

UNWRAPPING OUR CHRISTMAS GIFT 103

WHO KILLED JESUS? 104

GOOD CONDITIONS FOR CREATIVITY 105

GOD BLESS OUR ENEMIES 106

MERCY ON WHEELS 107

THE DAY AND PLACE, THE DEVIL CRIED 108

THE FIRST EASTER PARADE 109

THE INTER—FAITH ATTITUDE 110

THE LOCAL CHURCH CAN NOT BE REPLACED 111

GO TO THE ANT, THOU SLUGGARD AND BE WISE 112

THE MOST IMPORTANT QUESTION .113

THE NATURE OF OUR LOSTNESS 114

THE PAYLOAD HAS LANDED 115

THE POWER OF RECOMMENDATION 116

THE PREACHER, A TREE 117

WHY ONLY HAPPINESS WHEN WE COULD HAVE JOY? 118

WHOSE BIRTHDAY IS IT? 119

WHY DOES OUR FATHER FORBID LYING? 120

WHO WILL YOU BELIEVE? 121

WHERE IS YOUR TREASURE? 122

WHEN CHRISTIANS FAIL, WE MUST HELP 123

THERE IS BEAUTY FOR ALL AGES .124

THE RIGHT SIDE 125

LIFE AT ITS VERY BEST 126

LET'S GO FISHING WITH JESUS 127

LESSONS FROM KATRINA AND RITA .128

JESUS ANNOUNCES THE ELEVENTH COMMANDMENT 129

GIVE US THIS DAY OUR DAILY BREAD 130

GIVE AN ACCOUNT OF THY STEWARDSHIP 131

DEAD FLIES IN THE OINTMENT 132

CHRISTIANITY PROVIDES LIVING POWER 133

CHRISTIANITY OFFERS PERSONAL SOVEREIGNTY 134

A MOST WORTHY REQUEST 135

A HAND POINTING UPWARD 136

A FISH SWALLOWS A PREACHER 137

WHY STAND YE GAZING INTO HEAVEN? 138

MAKING GOD LOOK BAD 139

WHO IS THE BIGGEST FOOL? 140

WE ARE ALL ON A JOURNEY OF CHANGE 141

TRUE COURAGE IS LIKE A KITE;
A CONTRARY WIND RAISES IT HIGHER 142

TO OUR OLDER MOMS: THE GRANDS,
GREATS AND GREAT GREATS 143

THE DIRECTION AND PROGRESS OF JESUS 144

THE PAPARAZZI AND US 145

THE CALL TO SAINTLY LIVING 146

THE BIBLE IS GOD'S BOOK OF STANDARDS 147

THE ABSOLUTELY NECESSARY INGREDIENT 148

RISING ABOVE PETTINESS 149

PENANCE IS NOT NECESSARY 150

LIFE IS LIKE A TREE 151

JESUS REVIEWS HIS CHURCHES 152

IF WE GO FOR HIM, HE WILL GO WITH US 153

THE NINE BEATITUDES OF JESUS, CONTEMPLATED 154

FINE TUNING AND REDEDICATING OUR LIVES 155

WHAT TYPE OF WORSHIP PLEASES OUR FATHER? 156

CROSS CARRYING 157

WE MUST ALL BE STUDENTS AND TEACHERS 158

WE ARE ALL PREACHERS 159

TRACKING WITH JESUS—GRAVE TO HEAVEN 160

TOTAL HONESTY—WHY NOT? 161

TO EVERYONE, A CROSS 162

THE GREATEST TRUST AND ASSIGNMENT 163

THE BEST NEWS IS THE GOSPEL NEWS 164

PORNOGRAPHY IS BAD BECAUSE 165

ANGER + D = DANGER 166

ADVICE TO THOSE LIVING ON RESIDUAL GRACE 167

NEW YEAR, OLD STORY 168

THE SERMON ON THE MOUNT 169

THE RENT VEIL 170

THE REACH OF GOD 171

THE MAKING OF SAINTS 172

OUR FATHER WANTS US TO SUCCEED 173

SEX EDUCATION 174

MORE THAN CONQUERORS 175

LIFE IN BALANCE 176

HIGH NEED, LOW COMMITMENT 177

ADAM'S APPLE 178

ACCOUNTABILITY 179

ONE FOR THE "CRITTERS" 180

ALL ABOUT A CONNECTION 181

ONE RED ROSE 182

WHATEVER HAPPENED TO SIN? 183

GOD'S ORDER 184

IS THIS YOUR FINAL ANSWER? 185

LAW AND GRACE 186

OUR FATHER WANTS US TO BE FRIENDLY 187

POWER FAILURE 188

SCIENCE AND RELIGION 189

SUN, STAND STILL 190

THE ORDINARY THINGS 191

MY GENERATION IS FAST SLIPPING AWAY 192

THE PEACEMAKERS SHALL BE CALLED
"THE CHILDREN OF GOD" 193

LET HER ALONE, SHE HAS DONE WHAT SHE COULD 194

THE GREATEST INVITATION 195

RELIGION OF THE HEART 196

THE GREATEST CALL 197

THERE ARE PRISONS WITHOUT BARS 198

THY WILL BE DONE 199

BUILD YOUR HOUSE UPON THE ROCK 200

THE GRACE OF GOD IN ME STORED 201

THE COST AND JOY OF COMMITMENT 202

TWO BLIND MEN HELPED ME TO SEE 203

I BELIEVE IN GOD AND
I HAVE DECIDED TO BE A WITNESS 205

LIFE'S SUPREME PURPOSE

Jesus gave us what must be life's supreme purpose: "Seek ye first the kingdom of God and His righteousness and all these things shall be added unto you." There will be secondary goals but this must be supreme! Because our priorities are right, subordinate goals will be achievable (shall be added...) When our secondary goals leave their subordination to the kingdom of God, their joys and pleasures will soon sour and some will turn into the bitterness of gall. IF WE FAIL TO SUBMIT TO THE RULE OF THE KINGDOM, IF THINGS ARE WRONG AT THE CENTER OF LIFE, THINGS WILL BE WRONG AT THE FRINGE OF LIFE.

The great American problem is that we have been giving ourselves to secondary things, first. The news carries evidence everyday that many have lost their sense of the vitals. If we live everyday in deep quest for and strong dedication to the kingdom of God and His righteousness, we will live life at the highest level with its greatest accomplishments, its purest joy and lasting rewards, As with Adam, God is still going to the garden of our dedication and calling out, "_____, WHERE ARE YOU?" We know Adam's answer. What is ours, yours? (Matthew 6:33).

YOU ARE FREE TO SUCCEED

Your worst enemy, my friend, is not the devil, not his imps whom they say stalk us night and day. There is enough and more on the other side to counter that. There are no stars under which you are born, which pre-determined a course of failure or success which will ensue. We have no enemies on high with the power to point you out in a crowd and yell out: "Hey you there, you're a loser by decree. I don't care about your breaks, fold it up kid; you are beat, you're marked for defeat."

Success in your enterprise depends somewhat on chance or plight, a bit on the times, but what will tilt the scales, my friend, is beyond the reach of these, it is in you. Ah...it is there that battles are won or lost. The key to success is in your ability to be inspired, to respond, to bounce back, and to keep your head when cursed or blessed.

So get hold of yourself; flush out those leaches which sap the strength of body, soul, and mind. Cultivate clear channels through which to communicate with your God, your fellow-man and not the least with yourself.

HE WHO HAS EARS TO HEAR

Human ears are multiple in purpose and use; they give us balance, looks and some of us find them useful to hang things on, like glasses and jewelry. Jesus indicates that not all are making full use of our receptive organs; He says, "He who has ears to hear, let them hear." He likens those who hear and obey "those sayings of mine, unto a wise man who built his house upon a rock." (Matthew 7:24-29).

The deep things of God come to those who strongly desire His will and guidance. God speaks to us in a variety of ways and tones, sometimes with the voice of thunder but frequently in the still small voice. The listening ear, which is in tune with the heart of God, will hear Him in sound advice, ministry, those who cry or laugh, the church, the Bible, life experiences and directly from the Holy Spirit.

An 18th Century Christian, William Law, advises, "The highest you can seek, the best you can obtain, can be nothing higher or better than this—the light of God rising on the soul and resting there. Begin with this at once and carry it with you all along." Christians who stay in a constant receptive mode have experienced the "Author" and will also experience the "Finisher" (refiner) of our faith. (Hebrews 12:2).

PRACTICING THE SACRAMENT OF LIVING

A foolish man said, "I don't mix religion and business."
We make a serious mistake when we divide our lives into two
kinds of functions; that is "sacred or religious" and "secular or
common".

We may trust God in religious activities and conduct the
ordinary affairs of life with far less awareness and dependence
on Him. There, we may function by our wits and native
abilities but God wants to have part in all we do. The Bible
says, "Whether therefore ye eat or drink or whatsoever ye do,
do all to the glory of God." (1 Corinthians 10:31). By
selecting two of the most ordinary activities, "eating or
drinking" and putting them into a sphere of God
consciousness and service, we are to understand that our
whole life should be sacramental.

Bible reading, prayer, church attendance and all the
formal sacraments of the church are religious matters but so
should be every other activity of the Christian life. Those who
walk two different roads and must continually cross
over as the occasion dictates can get mixed up; they may
sometimes forget to be practical on Sunday and religious
on Monday. Practicing the sacrament of living will assure
us God's continual presence, breathe in us a sense of
accountability and give us a healthy awareness of others.

TRIAGE (SORT OR CHOOSE)

A local hospital notice reads: "All patients seeking treatment in the Emergency Dept...will be triaged first by a registered nurse... you may have to wait a long time." I had left my cup of coffee and drove a friend there at high speed, lights blinking, confident that traffic and police would understand. All babies and some adults know about Triage and exploit it with fussing and crying which reaches the crescendo of fits, knowing they will get first attention.

We need to apply the principle of Triage in the affairs of our lives. A "not so untypical" order may be: pleasure, money, status, friendship, family, church, and God's will. Such an order screams for responsible Triage. Any order which does not begin with God is an "out of order". Where are you? "What shall it profit a man if he shall gain the whole world and lose his own soul?" What is your life? These three Bible questions address our position, value and quality of life. They go beyond instant and temporary gratification taking into consideration our final judgment and eternal values.

OH, GOD, SAVE US FROM MISMANAGED AND UNBLESSED LIVING—FROM "MAJORING ON MINORS AND MINORING ON MAJORS!" (Matthew 11:28-30). He will always give you all you need from day to day if you will make the kingdom of God your primary concern. (Luke 12:31 LNT).

ARE YOU A GIVER, A GETTER, OR BOTH

Jesus said, "It is more blessed to give than to receive." Moffett translates, "It is happier to give than get." Jesus constantly made reference to opposites: the ready-not ready, broad-narrow road, alive-dead, rock-sand foundations, givers and receivers. We all give and receive but He tries to call attention to our predominant passion.

Judas' passion for getting became so over-developed that he went to Jesus' enemies and asked, "What will you give me if I deliver Him to you?" (Matthew 26:15). He may have reasoned that, "Jesus will get out of it and I will get a lot of money!"

We all have been getters since our first baby cry, demanding food or comfort. That was normal then but some still cry and have not become givers. There are people all about who are suffering severe financial, health, moral, loneliness, or family problems. The giving person sees the need and helps. The Bible speaks of what motivated Jesus to give His very life for us and continues to give: "Looking to Jesus, the author and finisher of our faith, who for the joy that was set before Him endured the cross, ignoring the shame..." Seeing what His cost would buy for us made it all bearable! Bible religion seeks to make us gracious receivers and generous givers! (Hebrews 12:2).

CHOOSE THE RIGHT SIDE, ALWAYS

A free society puts a heavy responsibility on us to choose. Before we take a side, our first thought and prayer should be, "Which is God's side?" We may have to disappoint some nearest and dearest to us and frequently stand with the few. God and His blessings are always on the side of honesty, truth and fairness. Nothing can endure very long without these qualities, for they must stand without practicality and God's blessings.

Right will be challenged and may suffer set-backs but will win in the end. Right's temporary losses are better than wrong's gains because God is always with those who strive to do what is right. The Bible speaks, "God blesses those people who refuse evil advice and won't follow sinners...The Lord is with everyone who follows Him."

Right may be slower than evil because it doesn't take shortcuts nor employs unethical practices and those who hitch their energies to it will win; it is practical and God's power is committed to its process. However, right loses power when the ingredients of intolerance and impatience become part of the mix. Right will make herself known to all who love and respect her and the heavens are instructed to carry the blessings of God there. (Psalms, Chapter 1).

ALL A LITTLE BIT CRAZY

The greatest benefits and disappointments occur in interpersonal relationships. Six of God's Ten Commandments are designed to help us with our relationships. We can handle the inanimate problems much more easily than those which arise out of two or more people who "step on each others toes".

These conflicts are everywhere, in the home, the workplace, the neighborhood, and even the church. While none of us are without wonderful contributive equalities, we seem to have a little craziness and one's craziness ignites another's. Clashing bitterly over minor things and ignoring the benefits of togetherness is a major human fault.

While Jesus was suffering major abuse, He kept on saying, "Father, forgive them, they don't know what they are doing." Those who can ignore absorb or forgive the faults of others are the happiest and are more likely to succeed and have their own faults overlooked and forgiven. (Matthew 6:12). Most of what God gives us comes through others like us, earthen vessels, un-polished, part-wrong and a little bit crazy. Those who are at peace and actively help others live peacefully. Peacemakers are called, "The Children of God." (Matthew 5:9).

CONGRATULATIONS TO ALL THE GRADS

Genius without an education is like gold in the mine. You make us proud! Your school has declared you ready to enter the market or profession or the next school of your choice. You are not wasting time when you are "sharpening your ax." If you keep up with progress and developments, each year you will wonder how you lived in last year's ignorance; you must never stop learning.

Be a teacher to all who will hear you and a student to all who will teach you! Cultivate friendship and let your greatest rivalry be not with your friends but with your own record, always trying to do better and to be better! Live in truth, if you make a mistake, admit it quickly; fix it, don't try to cover it up. The greatest book ever written says, "BUY THE TRUTH AND DON'T SELL IT."

Keep a compassionate ear and eye for the less fortunate; you may be blessed so you can help them. There is something vulgar about plenty and need living side by side; you must help them average out. God has not given us anything for our own consumption alone. Seek not only to please your employer; your dedication and quality of work should meet God's standard, wanting to please Him will bring out the best in you. He, more than any, has invested in us and it will be His saying, "WELL DONE" at the end which matters most!

Dog—Gone Happy

I walked out of my back door, bowed low in spirit. Multiple problems had joined forces to cast a dark cloud over my horizon, as dark as a Kuwaiti oilfield. The distance, I could see clearly, was very short indeed; menacing fears clawed at my peace of mind.

At that moment, I was met by my two dogs who were happy as "all-get-out". Pepper had been run over three times by cars, snake bitten and in her three years, needed medical attention a half dozen times. Coyote was dropped off as a puppy and I just let him stay. Today, none of this matters—they ran circles, jumped over each other, competed for a chance to lick my fingers and tried to lead me into an exciting field trip. Their attitude was contagious and I soon became positive again.

A wise man mused, "I am not as concerned about the 'wolfishness of the wolf as with the sheepishness of the sheep'". Most defeats are within, where the spirit breaks and then our whole reservoirs of power follow. The Bible advises, "Think about things that are pure and lovely and dwell on the fine, good things in others. Think about all you can praise God for and be glad about." IF WE AREN'T PICKY ABOUT WHO OR WHAT PREACHES TO US, GOD WILL SEND US HELP. (Philippians 4:8 LNT).

FREEDOM IS A DOOR FOR GOOD OR EVIL

If there is a God, why does He allow so much sorrow, pain, hunger, injustice and war? This is the question I most often hear as people attempt to relate an all-powerful God to a world full of trouble. The God they want would somehow make everything turn out alright, although we may live selfishly and ignore His rules for living. We don't realize that to give us the world we want, He would have to take away our freedom.

In our present world, room can not be made for good without also leaving the door open for evil. Neither God nor we want to impose such rigid protection on our children. Such insulation would reduce us to robots or like checkers moved on a board, void of initiative. The tree from which Adam and Eve chose to eat (direction they chose to go) bears "good and evil fruit."

Some among us have given God the pleasure of fine-tuning their lives to become the "salt of the earth, light of the world..." (Matthew, Chapter 5-6). Others have gone the full distance of depravities fall. They have used, and some will continue to use, God's gifts to hurt others. Yes, God could have an evil-free world if He chose but it would be void of "voluntary good"; it might even be boring. Let us not add to our present troubles, the sin of blaming God for the September 11, 2001 tragedy. CHOOSE GOOD!

GIVE DAD A FEELING

We want to first of all give honor to the Father of us all! The greatest privilege on earth is to be able to call the Creator of heaven and earth "OUR FATHER"! Knowing the importance of being properly related to God and the family, a wise father wants to see his children adopting Christian values and developing socially and ethically. He reviews his children and sighs with joy or grief.

More than any gift on Father's Day, Dad wants a "feeling", a sense that the kids are turning out alright. Fathers who are themselves obedient sons of Our Heavenly Father find it easier to establish good and easy relationships with their own children. The important lessons of life must be passed down to the children; life is too short and the lessons too costly for each to learn all first-hand. The maintenance of good communications and healthy respect for everyone in the family will help to transmit the wisdom and experience of age to the young, and youth will make its own vital contributions!

On Dad's special day, give HIM a feeling! Give Dad that priceless, yet affordable gift: A GOOD FEELING ABOUT THE COURSE OF YOUR LIFE FROM HERE ON!

Give Thanks with a Grateful Heart

The first New England Thanksgiving was celebrated less than a year after the Plymouth Colonists had settled in the new land. After a dreadful winter and loss of nearly half the colony, a bountiful harvest raised their morale and they were thankful!

From birth to death, our enjoyment and accomplishments should be tempered with deep gratitude, first to God and then to all who by God's grace contribute to their experience. Everything we enjoy, know or own has other people's stamp of contribution on it. A sure sign of maturity is that we do not forget to give thanks and are not devastated or distracted when others forget to thank us. We must not lose our dedication to service and generosity, even if nobody says, "Thank you." Jesus, taking bread, gave thanks, broke it and gave it to His disciples and said: "...This is my body which is given for you..." (Luke 22:19).

If He, our great example, the one sacrificed, could give thanks, how much more we—the recipients of the benefits of that awesome sacrifice—should be giving thanks day and night! May we be aware and openly thankful to those people who effect our daily lives by duties they may be hired to do and by the "beyond duty" attitude and services that they render. Let us catch up with our "THANK YOU, DEBT" and purpose to stay current! (Romans 1:21).

Let's Join the Witness Team, Today

We have been following the news of two American girls who were arrested for breaking Taliban law. The charge: TELLING THE PEOPLE ABOUT JESUS' LOVE. If we were accused of being intense witnesses for Jesus, could we honestly plead guilty?

I admire Mary and Joseph's submission and dedication, the enthusiastic angels who announced His birth, the shepherds, the wise men who traveled far to worship Him! Their witness was about a baby, a beginning of the Father's wonderful redemptive plan for us all. We now have much more to announce and report than they, the complete gospel (good news) to proclaim! We can report of Jesus' death, burial, resurrection, ascension and the Holy Spirit who came to help us! We know of the grace of God at work in the human soul, of sins forgiven and the indwelling Spirit changing us, qualifying us, making us laborers together with God. (1Corinthians 3:9).

We are asked to join Mary, Joseph, the angels, shepherds, wise men, apostles, saints past and present and the American "Aid Workers", Heather and Dayna, to be like "His star" who led people to Jesus. Today is the best time to begin to give Jesus our everyday, constant, enthusiastic witness by word and example! HOW COULD WE NOT DO IT?

Our Christian Power Source

Suddenly, with sound as of a rushing, mighty wind and strange phenomena, the Holy Spirit came! Jesus had told them He would not leave us orphans or comfortless. (John 14:16-26). That grand entry of special energy from heaven would be the Holy Spirit's contribution to breathe spiritual life into the lost and to energize the whole structure and witness of the church.

It was not an initiation rite but The Holy Spirit had come to stay for as long as the church would be on earth. The instructions to be filled with and to walk in the Spirit are not optional—vital Christianity does not function, indeed, cannot function unless it is lived, practiced and promoted at Holy Spirit pitch. As the offices of Father and Son were indispensable in conceiving and accomplishing the groundwork of our redemption, the Holy Spirit is necessary to power and apply this heavenly remedy.

The serious Christian's responsibility is to keep his or her life continually and immediately plugged into God's power source. Out of this relationship will emerge victorious and successful living! They will live in all Christian adequacies, "BE MORE THAN CONQUERORS, HAVE A STRONG WITNESS AND GO FROM GLORY TO GLORY." (Romans, Chapter 8; Acts, Chapters 1-2).

PATIENCE IS A NECESSARY
LIFE INGREDIENT

Our push-button, hurry up and instant mentality leaves us poorly prepared to cope with the stubborn and slow moving chores of life. How very foolish, wasteful, cruel, dangerous and impatient life can be; it releases all the negatives and the bad in us. No wonder, Jesus said, "In your patience you possess your souls."

Wonderful goals and dreams have been lost for lack of patience. Many friendships and marriages have failed because "the impatient pressed too hard and too fast." We need patience with each other, with ourselves, with God and especially, God with us. The Bible lists three ways by which patience may be acquired: First, the good examples of those who suffer and wait inspire us (James 5:10); Second, "tribulation works patience" (Romans 5:3). Our exposure to extended problems develops an ability to endure. Third, it is a gift or fruit of the Holy Spirit. "The fruit of the spirit is love, joy, peace, patience, gentleness, goodness, faith, meekness, self control." (Galatians 5:22-23).

The life which has come into full Christian provision will be progressive and patient in proper blend. Thomas Edison said, "Everything comes to him who hustles while he waits." The Bible states, "For ye have need of patience, that after ye have done the will of God, ye might receive the promise." (Hebrews 10:36).

THE DEEP CALLS UNTO THE DEEP

The deep of God calls to us and our own yearnings call for "DEEP REALITY" in our spiritual life. There is in all of us a vacancy in the shape of God. We may cram other things in there but only God can fill and satisfy His place.

The Bible abounds with calls to intimacy with God and invites us into a deep walk and working of the Holy Spirit in our own soul. The prophet Ezekiel was shown the quality of God's power and help in a vision of a stream which originated at God's Temple and continually progressed in depth and influence to the Sea. The waters brought healing and caused vegetation and fish to flourish in abundance. The healing stream was measured at ankle, knee, waist and over the head depths as it progressed.

We reveal the extent of our participation with God—our conduct, discipline and attitude, like "water marks" show what part has been touched by God's healing. There are the ankle, knee, waist and deep water Christian. Everything about us, which doesn't have God's mark, carries other marks of influence-inferior, debilitating and dangerous. Our Father offers us deep religious life which saves us for heaven later and also for earth, now! IT IS SAD THAT SOME PEOPLE HAVE ONLY ENOUGH RELIGION TO MAKE THEM MISERABLE. Hmmm—better be checking the marks of our religious life. "Don't copy the behavior and customs of this world but be a new and different person with a fresh newness...then you will learn from your own experience how His ways will really satisfy you." (Romans 12:1-2 LNT).

THE GOLDEN RULE CONTEMPLATED

I would like for others to be patient, kind, understanding and to not take advantage or exploit me. I want compliments in success and firm but gentle correction in error. In my absence, friends would defend me and all would laugh with me but not at me. I don't want church or sales people to treat me as a project but be helpful, never violating my free will. I would like to be given quality time to hear me out, to meet me at my level of grasp, not leaving me intimidated. I would like those who are richer, wiser, more educated, more profound, more religious, as well as those over whom I may excel, to be my friends. I want fair treatment, not on the basis of race, color, religion, gender or money. I want fun but also sincere conversation, not "brush-off" surface talk, repeating if necessary, without raising their voices. I want to be told the truth. I would like to feel friendly vibes from all whose paths I cross—a "nod" or a "hi", "nice day!" I don't want to be avoided but to feel human love and care which translates into, "I see you, you count; together we'll win!" If this is how I want to be treated, this is how I must treat all others. THE HOLY BIBLE, THE GOLDEN RULE. (Matthew 7:12).

THE ORDINARY THINGS OF LIFE

Normal living is made up of long stretches of very ordinary activities with an occasional "super-happening." It is in conducting those common activities that success or failure results. All accomplishments, whether dedicating a building, signing a document or receiving an award, have been preceded by days, weeks, months or years of common labor.

Also, for the most part, our religious experiences are not something we might "write home about." Christianity has very little record of fantastic happenings. Very few have walked on water, seen angels or been to heaven and back, as Paul. Most have not had "earth–shaking experiences" and yet we are sure of our faith and it works well.

Those who thrive on the spectacular will soon be disappointed because God distributes those in limited measure and only for good reasons. His power is always at work in the ordinary chores of life! God's specialty is the transforming of defeated and mismanaged lives into wholesome order. "I came that they may have life and have it more abundantly." (John 10:10). All who will open the ordinary affairs of their lives to God's "Son-shine" will see clearly and succeed with living! Those succeeding lives will, in turn, help to ignite the life of God in others who will positively affect still more! (Matthew 28:18-20).

THE SWORD OF THE LORD
AND OF GIDEON

Our nation's sense of right and wrong was originally based on Bible principles whose values are rooted in the Ten Commandments and further defined by the Christian gospel and letters to the churches. The first four are said to be "vertical" in focus; they address our responsibility to God. The last six are "horizontal"; they tell us how we should treat each other. There is not one telling us to watch out for ourselves.

Obviously, there is enough built-in "watch out for self" in all of us. In fact, most of the laws we write are designed to keep us from violating others in our drive to please ourselves. God's rules for living are as reasonable as traffic lights and danger signs; who can argue with them-they are for our own good! All His instructions are given to us by a loving Father who wants the very best for us all. We will always benefit if we obey and always lose if we ignore them.

More than anything else, our country desperately needs to recapture our sense of right and wrong and to reaffirm that we are A NATION UNDER GOD. Then, we will be able to announce with Gideon, "The Sword of the Lord and of Gideon." We must do all we can to dismantle this 9/11 terrorist enemy and the best place for us all to start is to read and implement this Bible verse: (2 Chronicles 7:14).

THE GREAT IMPERATIVE

When asked, "Why do you preach so much about, you must be born again," George Whitefield said, "Because you must be born again." Born again (born from above) is a phrase coined by Christ to describe the change which begins at the moment we cease to walk away from Him and we accept His help. Our sins are forgiven and spiritual life begins a process by which the Holy Spirit enables us to reposition our priorities and to adopt the will and purpose of Christ.

The transformation begins in the spirit and works outward through the mind, the will, emotions and the body, sanctifying and setting right the whole person. This conscious regeneration is not by merely joining a church, nor by reformation, but new life from the Holy Spirit which can transform the vilest sinner into the holiest saint. Born again does not mean instant maturity any more than babies are at once mature; we must not confuse the new birth with maturity, nor doubt it for lack of maturity.

Christ's words, "You must be born again" were spoken to the most religious and refined of His day; therefore, the need to be born from above is universal and without exception. Jesus said, "You must be born again." There is no other way or remedy. (John 3:1-18).

THE GOSPEL, CONTEMPLATED

Religion takes on varying forms of emphases as it passes through mortal hands and human interpretation. Some make it rigid and hard while others accept little or no responsibility to trim their lives by its laws. Many explain away its miracles and values while some strain the Scriptures to make them fit their purposes.

However, all views will stand before God's judgment and the verdict is always, LET GOD BE TRUE BUT EVERY MAN A LIAR. The greatest possible error is to believe that we alone could have no error. If Christianity fails us, it is always at the human level where we fail to grasp its message and its power. It seems that every generation needs its own "Sermon on the Mount" to realign teachings, adjust and SET US ON LIVE CENTER AGAIN.

The gospel does not go away; it finds us and calls by all possible means. Christianity originates deep in the heart of God and is practical for every generation. Jesus stood at our door yesterday and stands there again today, saying, "Let me in; I can help you; you need my help; I want to help you!" There are no disadvantages in opening our door to Him now! (Matthew 11:28-30).

Two Moms Sharing One Heart

I was privileged to read two letters, one from the mother of a heart donor and the other from the recipient of that precious gift. The mother of the fifteen year old writes of what he was, what he could have been and of this remaining piece of his life graciously shared. The recipient, the fifty-four year old grandmother employs the words: "Cried, Felt guilty, Grateful, Thankful and Sad for the family and especially the young life so soon gone."

Only those giving and those receiving can truly assess such value and with it the whole gamut of feelings which occupy their thoughts day and night. I have conducted many funerals and one of the most memorable is that of a young man of whom I was able to announce, "He is dead, yet he lives; his heart is pumping blood, his kidneys are filtering, his eyes are seeing and there are more body parts to be shared."

Jesus, who gave His life and body for all of us, must surely rejoice when we shared our witness of Him while living and also the usable remains of our body with others when we die. The "Two Moms Who Share One Heart" together promote: GIVE A GIFT OF LIFE.

WE ARE ALL CALLED TO SAINTLY LIVING

We are "called to be saints" (Romans 1:7) but we have pushed the idea as far away as possible, relegating it to the realm of the best dead Christians. The Bible words <u>Holiness</u>, <u>Sanctification</u>, <u>Spiritual Dedication</u> have become strange words to many Christians.

A business man said, "I don't mix religion with business." A pastor called for a show of hands by "All who have sinned last week." He followed, "Now I pray God will forgive you liars who didn't raise your hand." To what extent can the Christian live a Godly life in this modern world? The answer is, to the extent that he or she takes advantage of the provisions God has made for saintly living!

Paul writes, "...I plead with you to give your bodies to God. Let them be a living sacrifice, holy-the kind He can accept. When you think of what He has done for you, is this too much to ask? Don't copy the behavior and customs of this world but be a new and different person with a fresh newness in all you do and think. Then you will learn from your own experience how His ways will really satisfy you."
If Christianity fails us, it will be at the human level, where we fail to grasp its life, its power, and its discipline.
(Romans 12:1-2).

WE ARE ALL INVITED TO WALK WITH GOD

The Bible calls attention to a man named Enoch by saying that he "walked with God and God took him…" The Bible speaks very little about short-cuts around death and I don't know anyone who is counting on it except those who will be alive at Christ's return. Enoch must have experienced a most fulfilled life; the Bible leaves the details to our contemplation!

All who walk with God will move from discouragement to firm hope, from sadness to joyous living, failure to success, enmity to friendship, weakness to strength, and much more! Regrettably, we may be more interested in being saved when we die and less caring about developing a strong Christian life now.

Walking with God did not distract Enoch from normal work and responsible living but rather enhanced and equipped him for excellence. Our Father has no favorites; what is offered to one is offered to all. God wants to be with every one of us, day and night, to help us witness, be dedicated, prayerful, obedient, disciplined, and aware of His claim and our debt to others. He is calling to all of us by all means, "Let me walk with you, today, every day and I will teach you how to live; I will help you succeed; I will take you from glory to glory!" (Romans 12:1-2).

WE ARE THE BODY OF CHRIST

The Bible speaks of "The Body and Blood of Jesus" represented by consecrated bread and drink; our participation by eating and drinking is called "Holy Communion or the Lord's Supper." When we have grasped the significance of this devotion, we are ready to hear of another aspect of "The Body of Christ."

The whole of Christianity is likened to a human body with Jesus as head. There is no church without us and there can be no church without Christ who provided for, who calls, sends, enables and inspires. If the instructions originate with Christ and we faithfully minister, the Christian mission will be accomplished. The greatest tragedy is when we don't get involved or proceed on our own, independent of Christ or when strife within leaves us powerless.

Our Father trusts us with the gospel and its outreach is a necessary risk; He has no better help available to Him. God has set every member in the body as it has pleased Him. The ALL God wants to accomplish calls for ALL of us to do our part. The church is the most powerfully equipped force on earth when it maintains its contact with heaven. The highest call on earth is to be trusted with the gospel of heaven: LET US ENJOY THE PRIVILEGE AND TREMBLE UNDER THE RESPONSIBILITY. (1 Corinthians, Chapter 12; Revelation, Chapters 1-4).

Athens 2004:
Gold, Smiles, and Tears

We watched amazed as the Olympian contestants performed what seemed to us, super-human feats, but to them, mere routines. Humanity is a wonderful creation and endowed with marvelous abilities. We could not keep from feeling their quiet grief or exuberant joy as they went to their seats.

There was no room for error and that made it more inevitable that errors would occur. They had dedicated years of their lives with diligence and discipline and now a split-second of excellence or error would award them a medal of honor or cast them into the vast pool of the ordinary and mediocre. Considering the reputation and the aspiration of their coaches, families, peers and country, it seems too heavy a burden to carry.

However, our seeing the least of them in performance, reassures us that we can do whatever necessary thing we must do. We are beyond doubt, a marvelous creation, well-designed, well-formed and well-endowed by our CREATOR! The Bible speaks of an attainable and most worthy goal; in Christianity, there is room at the top for everybody!

Paul writes, "I have not yet reached my goal and I am not perfect, but Christ has taken hold of me. I keep on running and struggling to take hold of the prize . . . I forget what is behind and I struggle for what is ahead. I run toward the goal, so I can win the prize of being all he wants me to be and he saved me for. This is the prize which God offers because of what Christ Jesus has done." (Philippians 3:12-14).

CHRISTMAS IS ABOUT A FATHER'S SEARCH

Our first parents, exercising their free will, withdrew from God and we have added our own insults to the initial injury. Our frustrated lives, our breakdown in order and our shallow value systems reveal our problem. In our lostness, we do all kinds of crazy and hurtful things called sin.

Christmas is about our heavenly Father whose human family lost its way and His ingenious plan to restore us. Jesus, deity in human flesh, came with a proposal, a plan, right pleading with wrong. Christmas is about the condescension of Christ to accommodate and facilitate our reclamation and restoration. The plan for our recovery begun long ago would now, with rapid progress, bring Christ to us on that first Christmas morning. His life here, though short, would refocus our attention on true values, rip the veil of separation between God and man, pay our sin debt and fling open a door of access which we, in our sin, had closed.

In order to fully understand and appreciate the value and essence of Christmas, we must connect it with the other great events of Christendom—past, present, and future! We will then see that it is all about a Father's search for His family! ONLY WE CAN STOP HIM FROM SAVING US. (John 3:16-19).

DRIVEN BY LOVE

Knowing that horrible treatment and death awaited Him, Jesus proceeded toward Jerusalem and the cross on the day now known as Palm Sunday.

Arresting officers took Him to the former High Priest, Annas, who assessed and sent Him to the present High Priest, Caiaphas. There He was horribly interrogated and mob action was generated against Him. He was sent to the Roman Governor. Pilate, anxious to avoid the ordeal, sent Him to King Herod who mocked Him with robe and staff and a crown of thorns and sent Him back to Pilate who did his best to appease the worked up mob by offering to crucify a vicious criminal instead. The mob, with its collective evil mind made up, shouted, "Crucify Him" and threatened Pilate.

At the various trials, Jesus could have gotten out, but His love for us drove Him on as each trial became more severe than the previous one. Jesus ignored the call of those who loved and hated Him to "COME DOWN"; He remained until He could finally say, "IT IS FINISHED".

In the Temple, the very thick veil, which separated the people from where God was, became rent from "top to bottom". Access had previously been at an appointed day and by a certain person, but now open day or night, Sunday or Monday, we could personally go to Him.

The grave could not hold Him—He stood tall and defiant and announced, "Because I live, you shall live also". The Spirit of Christ (The Holy Spirit) now indwells His children who are spreading the Good News of His past, present and future—they are helping Him apply the benefits of the gospel (Good News) where they are needed. (Matthew 28:18-20).

Good News from the Graveyard

"...The chief priests and the Pharisees went together to Pilate. They said, 'Sir, we remember what that liar said while He was still alive. He claimed that in three days he would come back from death...' Pilate said, 'Take soldiers and guard the tomb as well as you know how!" So they sealed it tight and placed soldiers there to guard it.

Suddenly, a strong earthquake struck and the Lord's angel came down from heaven. He rolled away the stone, sat on it and announced, "HE IS NOT HERE! GOD HAS RAISED HIM TO LIFE JUST AS JESUS SAID HE WOULD..." Some soldiers who had been guarding the tomb told the chief priests everything that happened. The chief priests and leaders decided to bribe some soldiers with a lot of money. They said, "Tell everyone that Jesus' disciples came during the night and stole His body while you were asleep." The soldiers took the money and did what they were told. The people of Judea still tell each other this story.

Between resurrection and ascension, Jesus reassured the people by presenting Himself to many, in different places and circumstances. Jesus stood tall and defiant and announced to all who follow Him: "BECAUSE I LIVE, YOU SHALL LIVE ALSO." Those in whose heart the Spirit of Christ lives have the ultimate proof: "You ask me how I know He lives? He lives within my heart." (John 14:19; Matthew, Chapters 27, 28).

In Your Patience
Possess Ye Your Souls

Thieves in Amsterdam, Netherlands, made off with 20 paintings by Vincent Van Gough. The take was the largest art steal ever; included was "The Potato Eater", valued at millions of dollars. Fortunately, all the pieces were recovered, even with serious damage to some.

Van Gough's style was not appreciated during his life time; not even one piece sold. A lady even used one piece to stop up a hole in her chicken yard fence. His poverty kept him down and depressed and he became so frustrated that he cut off part of an ear to make a statement. The world took its time to appreciate the impressionist's creativity, time which Van Gough ran out of; he took his own life with a gun in 1890.

Some people live with an abnormal preoccupation about their worth. They are always measuring themselves by imaginary standards of timing and often compare themselves with others in order to feel good about themselves.

Most of what we do requires an incubation, maturation and acceptance time. Jesus said that the growth of the kingdom is like a seed sown and eventually the immature ear, then finally the mature ear of corn. He said, "My meat is to do the will of Him that sent me and to finish His work." The Bible says, "Whether therefore ye eat or drink or whatsoever you do, do all to the glory of God. And whatsoever ye do, do it heartily as to the Lord and not unto men." Paul said He DIDN'T CARE ABOUT CREDITS OR CONDEMNATION, IT WOULD BE GOD'S JUDGEMENT IN THE END WHICH WOULD COUNT. (Colossians 3:23-24).

LORD TEACH US TO PRAY

A mom asked Jesus, "In your kingdom, please let my two sons sit one on either side of you." Two disciples who became known as "The Sons of Thunder" asked Him to call down fire on those who were not receptive to His ministry.

Neither petition was granted and Jesus pointed out their error. He will not grant ill-conceived requests and for that reason we should always end our petition with, "Thy will be done." Seeing the value of prayer, one of His disciples asked, "Lord teach us to pray..." Jesus said, "After this manner pray...Our Father, who art in heaven, hollowed be Thy name. Thy kingdom come. Thy will be done in earth as it is in heaven. Give us this day our daily bread. And forgive us our debts, as we forgive our debtors. And lead us not into temptation but deliver us from evil; for Thine is the kingdom and the power and the glory, for ever, Amen..." (Matthew, Chapter 6).

In this model prayer He teaches us what acceptable and effective prayer consists of—the substance and attitude of kingdom praying. If we can say "Our Father" at the beginning, we should be able to say "Amen" (so be it) at the end of the prayer! When we don't pray, we are saying—"I don't need you Father..." With answers in hand, Our Father waits, and longs to hear us pray!

Open The Door—Dummy!

Jesus speaks to the Laodiceans, "Look, I have been standing at the door and I am constantly knocking. If anyone hears me calling him and opens the door, I will come in and fellowship with him and him with me… You say that I am rich; I don't need a thing! You don't realize that spiritually you are wretched and miserable and poor and blind and naked…"

Oh, the tragedy of living only the turn of a door knob away from the help we so badly need. Jesus knocks at the door of our heart day and night, in gain and loss, health and sickness, good and bad examples, by song, sermon and the Holy Spirit's own appeal. The great danger is that we will run out of time or become hardened and no longer hear His knock and call.

His call carries a tone of urgency—it is a hurry-up call. Even in hell, He will still love us but we will be beyond the reach of His help. The Bible laments the plight of those who never open to Christ's knock, whose window of opportunity is wasted and lost: "The harvest is past, the summer is ended and we are not saved." That is the ultimate failure and tragedy. He wants to forgive our sins, give us the Holy Spirit to be our personal helper, give us a church family, enhance our life now and for eternity! ISN'T IT DUMB TO NOT OPEN THE DOOR OF OUR LIFE TO HIM? (Revelation 3:14-22; Romans 10:6-13).

The Bible Call Is a "Hurry Up" Call

One of the most moving scenes in the Bible is Jesus' grieving over Jerusalem saying, "Oh Jerusalem, Jerusalem...how often I have wanted to gather your children together as a hen gathers her brood under her wings but you wouldn't let me and now your house is left desolate..." The Bible laments those who have not made peace with God, "The harvest is past, the summer is ended and we are not saved."

For everything in life, there is an appropriate time; we call it "a window of opportunity". This applies to everything about us: education, marriage, family, career and especially our salvation. King Agrippa, as judge, listened to the prisoner Paul's moving testimony and said, "You almost persuade me to become a Christian" but there is no record that he ever moved any closer than "almost".

"Almost" is never close enough—one either is or is not a Christian. Everywhere, in the Bible and human experience, there screams at us these words, "Now is the acceptable time; today is the day of salvation." The old song admonishes us with these words, "Don't let the door of mercy close on you..." There is every advantage and not one disadvantage in saying "yes" to God today. GOD'S CALL IS—"A HURRY UP" CALL!

There Is No Loss

Loss? You have loss, you say? There is no loss! Life is so full of interesting things to do, to see, to study that one should not weep for the loss of anything. One's loss merely frees him for involvement in another challenging and enjoyable enterprise. If we never lose or, by some other means, are forced out of an already explored area of interest; we would never have the pleasure of checking out something else. God's gift to us is a world so laden with goods that we will barely scratch its surface in a lifetime or even a thousand years.

If I become immobile, I will study what I now run over in my preoccupation. If I become poverty stricken, I will discover the ingenuity to survive which now lies dormant in me. If I lose my sight, I will further develop my other senses. If I lose my health, I will study the soul. If I lose friends, I will cultivate new ones. If I die, I shall enter into the presence of God. "All things work together for good . . . " (Romans 8:28).

The Bible Speaks To the Weak, the Poor, the Few

Much of the Bible is devoted to reassuring the weak, the poor and the few. A sense of weakness can be good because we may trust less in human resources and more in God's wisdom and power. Paul said, "My strength is made perfect in weakness...when I am weak then, I am strong." (2 Corinthians 12:9-10).

The Bible points to God's power and provision committed to us and says, "Let the poor say, I am rich; and the weak say, I am strong." The Bible further speaks, "Despise not the day of small things, be not weary in well doing for in due season, you will reap if you don't faint." Jesus said, "Where two or three are gathered together in my name, there am I in the midst of them." What does it mean, "...to be gathered in the name of the Lord?" If our endeavors originate with Him, if our attitude and motives correspond with the mission and mind of Christ, we are assured of His presence, His blessings and His power.

In His review of the seven churches of Asia, Jesus commended the poorest church and rebuked the richest one for its false sense of value. (Revelation, Chapters 1-3). We must be careful not to appraise value of our church by worldly standards. Whether we meet in a Cathedral or a stable is not important—the critical question is, "Is the Lord here with us?" A multitude or one plus the Lord is a majority!

THE CHRISTIAN REMEDY IS WITHIN

The people to whom Jesus first came rejected Him because He did not meet their expectations. They were looking for a leader who would free them from foreign rule. They understood their problem to be outside themselves.

Jesus said that our main problem is within the heart of every person. Among other things, our salvation lifts us up above nature's rule and into a reign based on God's will, love, consideration for others and harmony with God's purpose. In Adam, we slipped away from God and became controlled by influences which adversely shaped our value and conduct systems. THE SPIRIT WHICH CONTROLS OUR LIVES FORMS OUR UNDERSTANDING.

It seems reasonable to lie, cheat and steal when our motivation arises out of our depravity and evil influences. Jesus came to set up His kingdom in the heart by the indwelling Holy Spirit. He said that the kingdom of God in us would produce "righteousness, peace and joy in the Holy Spirit." Christ came to clear the way so that the life of God may reside in us. Unless we are fixed inside, we are not fixed at all and there will be occasions every day to demonstrate this truth. The Christian whose religion is like a heavy cross, too heavy to carry but is afraid to drop it lest he goes to hell, has not grasped Christ's message nor its power. (Romans 14:17).

THE GREATEST GIFT EVER GIVEN

Jesus said, "Fear not, little flock; for it is your Father's good pleasure to give you the kingdom." (Luke 12:32). The kingdom is everything of value under God's control and possession. It is His Salvation, Lordship and provision over and for us which doesn't run out. All who accept His Salvation have their sins forgiven and are given the family of Christ for kinship and fellowship and this is a true saying, "Blood flows thick but the Spirit flows thicker."

The Holy Spirit which is a measure of the life of Christ is part of our Salvation package. Jesus spoke with excitement when He told His disciples that a better arrangement was being made available to them described in these words, "I will pray the Father and He will give you another Comforter, that He may abide with you for ever...ye know Him and He dwelleth with you and shall be in you. I will not leave you comfortless; I will come to you...at that day ye shall know that I am in my Father and you in me and I in you...He shall teach you all things and bring all things to your remembrance...peace I leave with you, my peace I give you; not as the world giveth, give I you..." (John, Chapter 14).

Christ in us is our hope of glory; a life disciplined, productive, good for us, helpful and pleasing to our Father. His Salvation saves us for life on earth now and for heaven later. When Jesus cried out, "It is Finished," it signaled a most costly price to Him and a most wonderful gift to all of us, of joyous, helpful, victorious, enjoyable life on earth and a greater future which will have no negatives. The richest people are those who are in His kingdom, the poorest are those who have not opened their life to His continual knocking. (Romans 10:6-13).

THE POWER AND EFFECT
OF DEEP FEELINGS

"...Thy soul must overflow if thou another's soul would reach. It needs an overflowing heart to make the lips full speak..." The great accomplishments of our lives are those ideas we feel deeply about; those which make us cry, beg, work hard and awaken us at night. Most of the others die along the way for lack of the human spirit's contribution. We can convince others only to the extent that we feel about an issue.

The Christian message is enhanced or limited by our feeling of its importance. God is moved by prayers which are emotionally charged and prayed with a deep grasp of the importance: "The heartfelt and continued prayers make the tremendous power of God available to us." (James 5:16 AMP).

Our serious times call for committed people who care deeply, whose hearts burn and who speak emotionally! All others will be ignored, past by or lose interest. Christmas, Good Friday, Easter, Pentecost are all about feeling—God's feelings about us! The unfinished work of Christ is the application of the benefits of His passion where they are needed. The Bible based, Holy Spirit led, deep feeling witness will lead many to accept Christ's saving grace!

THERE IS GOOD NEWS FROM THE CROSS

"Because of His kindness you have been saved through trusting Christ and even trusting is not of yourselves, it also is a gift from God." (Ephesians 2: 8-9 LNT). The declaration of the greatest accomplished mission is Jesus' dying announcement from the cross, "IT IS FINISHED", leaving us to ponder His seven last sayings and what it all means to us!

At the same time, by God's initiative, the Temple veil was rent from top to bottom, not bottom to top. Thus came to us the forceful, visual announcement that now we may and can go to our Father, personally, day and night, in or out of church, Sunday or Monday! We would no longer need an appointed person to take our petitions to God for us, to an appointed place at an appointed time. God has announced an open door policy to all at all times! We all desperately need the salvation which our Father designed in heaven, Jesus paid for on earth and the Holy Spirit applies to the believers!

Matthew, Mark, Luke, and John were assigned by God to give us their first-hand, eye-witness accounts so nothing of importance would be left unnoticed and unreported of the life, ministry and passion of Jesus! WHO WILL YOU BELIEVE—"The Four Gospel Writers" or "modern-day would-be experts" who did not walk with Jesus then, nor knows Him now? (John 3:15-17; Romans 10:6-13; Matthew 28:18-20).

THEY NEED NOT DEPART

A multitude had followed Jesus into the wilderness and in the evening His disciples came to Him and said, "Lord, send them away to buy food, this is a desert place." He replied, "...They need not depart" and He miraculously fed more than 5,000. (Matthew 4:14-20).

Any church whose focus is on providing the "Full, Complete Gospel" (Good News) will certainly attract the Lord's focus and those who attend will see Him at work to make it happen. There could not be a greater church goal for this new year than to adopt "THEY NEED NOT DEPART" as their goal! Let all Christian virtues and power be dispensed to those in need who walk through Christ's sacred doors. Christ envisioned that His church, built upon the rock of His generosity, love, compassion and power would make it obvious to the needy that we need not look further for the gospel fully preached, fully practiced and fully applied.

The Revelation account of our Lord's review of the seven churches of Asia shows His frustration with the sad state of most of His churches there. (Revelation, Chapter 1-3). The list of His grievances are from the loss of their first love to false teaching to Satan occupying a seat to imperfect works to His having been grieved out of His own church and pleading for the door to be opened to Him. What can be said of our church, yours—He knows; ask Him, He will tell us. May each of us, together, help Jesus make the church we attend a place – caring, sensitive to needs, harmonious, cooperative and functioning in Christ's resurrection power, a place where the needy "NEED NOT DEPART."

WAS IT CHRISTMAS OR XMAS?

Did you have a Christmas or a Xmas celebration? Do you bristle up at the thought of substituting an X for Christ? The 4-letter word offends us terribly and yet, actions speak louder than words.

Join me, please, in honestly answering a few questions to determine if we have had a Christmas or an Xmas celebration: Did you openly recognize Christ's presence in your Christmas gatherings? "Where two or three are gathered in my name, I am there..." Was His name held high and often mentioned? Did you introduce your guests to the "Guest of Honor?" Was their Christ consciousness heightened in your home? As you ate from your bountiful supply, did you think about the hungry, the lonely and the lost? Could Jesus enjoy the spirit of your gathering or would He have been more at home, once again with the animals in the barn? DID WE HAVE A CHRISTMAS OR AN XMAS CELEBRATION?

If we could dishonor Him at His own birthday party, how much more we are apt to grieve Him in the ordinary affairs of our lives. Let us each purpose now, today, to be an everyday constant witness of all He has come to accomplish! The unfinished work of Christ is the application of the benefits of His passion where they are needed.

WHO IS JESUS—WHY DID HE COME?

Jesus has been called "The inescapable Christ"; He can not be ignored; He confronts us! We form opinions about Him; His disciples reported, "Some say that you are John the Baptist, some Elijah and others Jeremiah or one of the prophets." Others said, "He did miracles by the power of "the prince of devils." Some said, "He is an imposter and they felt they had to get rid of him" or "He is a good man who came to show us the way to God but that evil men killed Him and He was not able to do the work He came to do." The demonized, naked Gaderene, who lived among the tombs, begged Him, to leave because he perceived Him to be a hater of such men as himself. Peter said, "You are the Christ, the son of the living God."

The question of WHO IS JESUS continues to be pressed on all of us by circumstances, inner need and the ministry of the church, by the Bible and the Holy Spirit. The Bible calls Him "God in Christ" the Savior of all who will ask Him for help and adds that a day will come when every tongue will confess that He is Lord and every knee with bow to Him, as judge.

It is too bad that we would not bow and confess Him now when He could be our Savior. Becoming a forgiven, Holy Spirit filled, born again Christian is the greatest possible gain, the most available and easily obtained richness on earth. Jesus came to do this for us! (Act 2:37-41; Romans 10:6-13).

YOU HAVE NOT PASSED
THIS WAY BEFORE

The children of Israel stood on the east bank of the river; their oppositions were overcome one by one until only the Jordan River was between them and the Promised Land. They were instructed to, "Sanctify yourselves and follow the Ark of the Covenant, for you have not passed this way before..." (Joshua, Chapter 3). Following God's instructions, they crossed over into full access of the land God had given them.

Our journey through 2001 was especially eventful toward the end. September 11th (911) is a day of infamy, etched indelibly in our minds and emotions. It left us shaken and unsure but we are reacting well. We have identified the enemy and are confronting it. More people attended church the following Sunday than ever before and we are openly and unashamedly turning to prayer!

We must check the baggage of our spirit, soul and body, and with God's help lay aside everything which could hinder our life in the New Year. We must leave behind all hurt feelings, impure ambitions, prejudices and all attitudes contrary to our Father's will. Let us fill our lives with good and proper things. The Christ of Christmas and this year call out to all, saying, "Wear My Yoke—for it fits perfectly—and let me teach you..." All who will yoke up with Jesus will succeed with living! (Matthew 11:28-30).

You Must Like Yourself

I know of no man in whose presence I must bow low! I shared in the success of the refined and the lowly are part of me. We are all of the same clay, molded into individualities.

I have yet to see one person who would not have made him or herself a little different were they self-created. We all seem to have picked up some bum genes which are floating around in the bloodlines. We try to comb over, shorten, elongate, paint over or by other means minimize the impact of our flaws. It is regrettable that many spend their lives being very unhappy and not liking themselves. They focus on their negatives rather than on their many wonderful qualities.

God could not create such horrible creatures as some believe they are. The most important goal of the gospel is to help people be saved. However, "the good news from heaven" includes helping us be well adjusted and loving our life. Jesus came to save us for heaven and also for earth! The Golden Rule: "Do unto others as you would have them do unto you" implies our self-dignity. We cannot fully appreciate others until we like ourselves. A good intra-personal feeling breeds good inter-personal relationships. Do you want to do something very important? Help the people you meet every day to like themselves as God loves them! "...He will beautify the meek with salvation." (Psalms, Chapter 1; Psalms 149:4).

Jesus Knows

"As He stood in the Temple, He was watching the rich men tossing their gifts into the collection box. Then a poor widow came by and dropped in two small copper coins. Really, He remarked, this poor widow has given more than all the rest of them combined. They have given a little of what they didn't need but she, poor as she is, has given everything she has." (Luke 21:1-3). Jesus sees the offering and also knows how much we have left.

Show-off giving and praying in a manner designed to earn social points was strongly condemned by Jesus in His earthly ministry and is no less detested now. We are really only stewards of what God has entrusted to our care and distribution. Besides money, we need prayer, friendship, encouragement, support, acceptance, advice tolerance and more, in a context of love.

There is something vulgar about plenty and need, strength and weakness living side by side. If we are advantaged above others, we are to help level that difference. Jesus knows if we are completely honest stewards, doing our very best and with a pure motive. What we do for and to others, we are doing unto Him. If we have the mind and heart of Christ, like Him, we will be drawn toward the sights and sounds of need.

I KNOW SOMETHING
GOD HAS FORGOTTEN

I was just a little boy and was very mad at the lady next door. When she wasn't looking, I turned the hands of her clock wildly and set the clock back on the table. Later, she was awed by what time it was; I kept my silence. It was a child's angry prank but this much anger in an adult could have caused real havoc.

It is the first sin I remember committing and although I have repented, I have not forgotten it. However, we are told that the sins of the repentant are cast into "the sea of forgetfulness, never to be remembered against us!" God forgets but the Bible tells us to remember "the rock from which we were hewn and the pit from which we were dug." We are expected to make right our evil deeds and take responsibility for damages as much as possible, but the Bible clearly instructs us to accept our free forgiveness based on Christ's payment on the cross!

If we try to pay for our sins by other means, we are in fact, saying that Christ's sacrifice is not adequate. Our forgiveness puts a distance "as far as the East is from the West" between us and our forgiven sins! Let no one who has asked for Our Father's forgiveness continue to live under the weight of those sins. heaven has erased the record; let us also forgive ourselves and each other! (Psalms 86:5; Ephesians 2:4-9, 4:32).

I Called My Friend: "The Body"

The old must die and the young do die. A tragic accident occurred and a name listed sounded like my friend's name. I called the church and asked about him by name; the fear was justified, in an instant he was gone. My next call was to the funeral home and in the space of five minutes; I caught myself now referring to my friend as "the body."

How temporary, I thought, the Bible notes, "As a flower here today and gone tomorrow" or "as a vapor." Job noted that his life was passing "swifter than a weaver's shuttle." In view of our dependence on God, we are instructed to say, "If it is God's will, I will do this tomorrow…" If God withdraws His investment in us, we will immediately begin to return to dust.

At best, we are given a few years to develop our skills, secure our salvation and make our contribution. "Where death leaves us, judgment will find us and there eternity will hold us." How should we live and what should be our attitude in view of our temporariness on earth? King Solomon contemplated life from all angles and tested all of its possibilities. His studies ended with this recommendation: We should live kindly toward others and obediently toward God or else we will be very sorry at the end; we will have failed at living.

How to Avoid a Damaged Faith

There is insurance for most losses and yet the most important things are not insurable. No insurance can guarantee us health, peace, love and happiness.

I frequently talk with people whose religious faith is damaged; they are not so sure anymore about the Bible and absolute rules to live by. Some say, "What if, in the end, there is nothing to what I believe?" Many were severely disappointed by other Christians while more have not grasped the full essence and power of Christianity. Their faith has not grown to keep pace with the tests they now face or their own questions asked by a growing awareness.

As insurance must be added to cover increasing cost of replacement and services, so must we add to our basic faith to keep it current. The Bible speaks, "And besides this, (our basic faith) giving all diligence, add to your faith, virtue; and to virtue, knowledge; and to knowledge, temperance; and to temperance, patience and to patience... if you do these things... (continually add to your basic faith) ye shall never fall." Successful living is like riding a bicycle; we must keep moving forward or we will fall. (2 Peter 1:5-10).

HOSTAGE TO OUR HANG-UPS

Strong impressions chisel away at us as surely as the sculptor's chisel turns crude stone into an image. From the beginning of life, we are being molded into what we are becoming. We are a delicate and complex creation of spirit, soul and body which can rise to awesome heights and also descend to disgusting degradation and despair.

Considering that we were created to live in a "garden", it is no wonder that we are strained in our present environment. We were created with special capacities which equip us to communicate and function with Deity. Estrangement from our Creator leaves us vulnerable to evil and frustrations which only humans can experience.

Our times have produced a great need for counselors, shelters and support groups for the more impaired while many more go through life with an emotional limp. Our "chip on the shoulder", our "hang-ups" and "blind spots" adversely influence our interactions with others in all our social and economic activities. They strain relationships, influence decisions and make us unhappy. To all who are held hostage by fear, anger, low sense of worth, Christ says, "I have come that they might have life and that they might have it more abundantly." (John 10:10).

Happy Father's Day, Dads

The greatest privilege on earth is to be able to call God, The Creator of heaven and earth, Father. If, for the Father's Day celebration, we choose to head the list with the "Father of us all," it will not take away but enhance the occasion!

A multitude of titles, imagery and names involving the word "Father" are employed to help us grasp the qualities of our heavenly Father's love and commitment for us. Since the day He first breathed life into molded dust, we have been His special creation, made in His own image. The plan for our redemption from sin was conceived in His heart. He empowers us by the Holy Spirit to fulfill the role He has designed for us. He has given us the Bible, the church and family to sustain us. He is always attentive to our needs, our happiness and security; "every good and perfect gift comes from Him."

Within the context of our relationship, our Father wants to give us and our children success on earth and heaven for eternity. All fathers who will cultivate the relationship our Father wants with us will also have a better relationship with their own family. God knows that no one else can take our place in this important role. With answers in hand, He waits, yes longs for us to ask Him for help. He knows more than all of us about trials, needs and joys of Fatherhood! HAPPY FATHER'S DAY, DADS!

God's Grace

There is an oak tree in our backyard which has obviously been overshadowed by larger trees from its beginning. Its limbs are threaded out wherever they could find sunlight and room to grow; its top is not clearly defined, as if a big hand tried to hold it down all of its life. While its appearance is very different from its kind, it carries a special beauty, THE BEAUTY OF A SURVIVOR.

I have seen a lot of sadness, unavoidable trouble, pain and devastation. I've seen people die piece by piece over long periods of time. I've seen the innocent suffer under stress and others who inherited awesome crosses to bear. While we, the sympathizers may question, most of those suffering bear their problem with dignity and their faith is not shaken.

There is a distinguishing beauty about those who are deeply tried, those who must fully grasp the grace of God. We are a marvelous creation capable of accepting, adapting and overcoming! The Bible speaks, "Where sin abounds (or sickness, trouble, confusion) grace much more abounds." I salute the grace of God which from Him freshly flows when faith and prayer together tap its source but I now see grace more, the grace of God within me stored. We can do what we have to do!

A PRIVATE OR A SHARED FAITH

I heard it again, "My faith is very real and strong but it is private, something between God and me and I don't discuss it." Who can avoid speaking of such important matters as medical cures, social reforms and works of God in one's soul, home and church?

Maybe, when we carry a silent faith, we are saying it is a weak faith, one which isn't working well enough to excite or recommend. There is a vast difference between being a religious bore and being a responsible witness of eternal values; one is to be avoided, the other to be cherished and heard. Responsible sharers of the faith are teachers and also students to all, knowing that no one has exhausted the supply of God's grace. They are "reaching and pressing toward the prize of the high calling of God in Christ Jesus."

THE GOSPEL ACCORDING TO YOU; WITNESSED AND DEMONSTRATED WHERE PEOPLE LIVE, WORK AND PLAY IS THE MOST PRODUCTIVE. The people who most need the gospel do not usually attend church. How much do we need to know to be successful witnesses—exactly what you and I know now! "If your heart is on fire, there will be smoke in your eyes!" (Matthew 28:18-20).

NAME DROPPING

We may all be tempted to do a little name-dropping when the association promises to lift us up in the mind of our peers. Few can resist the temptation to brag about a handshake or autograph encounter with the notorious, the rich and famous. Some carry this to the ridiculous and become known as NAME-DROPPERS; many then lose credibility with those who really matter.

The great Apostle Paul, carried away with the value of knowing Jesus, did a lot of useful boasting, "I count everything else worthless when compared with the priceless gain of knowing Christ Jesus my Lord…" He had grasped experiential knowledge of knowing the Savior and he saw endless values now and for eternity. His immediate knowledge fed a yet greater desire to know Him fully, "I press toward the mark for the prize of the high calling of God in Christ Jesus."

No matter how advanced and developed we may be in Christian knowledge and experience, there remains a higher calling yet! No one has yet reached the pinnacle of the call of Christ which He has set before us! A bit of Christian boasting about knowing Jesus is in order and in fact, if He is not very much on our mind and in our conversations, we probably don't know Him very well. Our greatest possible tragedy on earth would be if we fail to know Jesus as Lord and Savior.

A Journey of Change

We are all on a journey of change; nobody remains the same. We are being molded by influences in and outside of ourselves. Everyday, good and evil are set before us and we make our choices. No force or power can make us do anything we are not willing to do; not even God will force His will on us but He will help all who ask.

We must take responsibility for what we are becoming. It is very sad to see someone becoming afraid, discouraged, suspicious, bitter, vengeful, mean and it is very refreshing to see others who are improving in similar circumstances. The Bible urges us to, "Fix your thoughts on what is true and good and right…"

Evil has not yet devised an approach which can corrupt a made-up mind but the unsettled mind and negotiable conscience will eventually give in to the corrupting forces. True religion, the one Jesus brought down from heaven and uncompromised by us, gives much greater power than all corrupting influence in our environment. The Bible speaks, "…There is someone in your hearts who is stronger than any evil teacher in this wicked world." (1 John 4:4; John 14:16-18 LNT).

A Silent Message on a Busy Day

I was hurriedly driving with a hundred things to do when I was suddenly stopped while a funeral procession slowly crossed our street. I nervously looked for a way around and out of the delay but there was no way out.

Then, I began to think of the deceased; we had been sojourners together. The votes we cast, the money, the prayers we prayed had made us participants in each other's life. I wondered if my fellow traveler had been properly presented God's plan of salvation, did he understand it, did he put it off or had he participated in God's commonwealth; was he fulfilled? I thought, "Where death leaves us, judgment finds us and there eternity will hold us."

I reviewed my own priorities and suddenly the things I wanted to do today didn't seem so important when measured by eternal values. King Solomon the Wise concluded that life is short, don't clutter it up; live by God's rules or you'll be sorry. I purposed to be more aware, kinder, more helpful, less selfish, more God aware, everyday. The procession now having passed through, I tilted my hat, whispered, "Hasta Luego, Revoir, See You Later" and we went each our way; he to his eternity and I to my preparation for it.

A Society with Predators

The most frightening thing about us is that we are fast becoming a society of predators. By mail, telephone, political platform, on the streets and sometimes even in a religious setting, we take by intimidation, threat and other unethical means what we want.

Life has become a cheap object to be overpowered or destroyed if it stands in the way of our greed and ambition. Small children are no longer safe at play; they can be picked up, abused, molested and killed to satisfy the adult with a disgusting appetite whetted by the merchants of erotic art and literature. We are becoming predators far worse than lower animal life. Our ability to reason makes us capable of falling into such depth of cruelty and vileness; it becomes an outrage to even call it beastial. When a person is at his worst, he is far worse than the beasts.

We are losing our fundamentals; we are building on sand. Thoreau said, "There are a thousand hacking at the branches of evil to one who is striking at the root." Will God punish us for forsaking Him and the ethics which are based on the Ten Commandments? He will not need to punish us; the direction of our ways carries its own built-in punishment. The Christian gospel seeks to develop everyone into a kind, compassionate and courteous human who does more giving than receiving. While some are choosing to go the whole distance of depravity's fall others are reaching for God's extended hand from heaven.

ALL KNEE-MAIL WILL BE ANSWERED

Our Father in heaven will answer all sincere "Knee-Mail Requests" of His Children; the answer will be "Yes, No or Wait a while." However, we should frequently approach Him without request, simply to tell Him, "Thank You" or to give Him praise and adoration and to present ourselves for His service.

Kneeling is a good and humble position in which to pray but there is no Bible precedent for only kneeling prayer. However, there is much said about attitude and position of the soul which seeks to be involved in prayer. A disciple, attracted to the power of prayer, petitioned Jesus, "Lord, teach us to pray…" Jesus' response to the request is recorded in Matthew 6:5-8; He begins by saying that some people don't pray the right way, "Don't be like them."

We should study the approach to and the contents of the model prayer to grasp what acceptable praying is like. It begins with "Our Father" and ends with "Amen" (so be it). It should not be hard to say "Amen" at the end if we can say "Our Father" at the beginning of the prayer. He says that if we ask, it will be given; seek and you will find; knock, and the door will open! Those who skim off the blessings without adjusting their lives to His will may discover that effective praying also calls for: "Humble yourselves. Seek My face and Turn from the wicked ways." God expects those who ask for kingdom blessings to walk in kingdom living. (2 Corinthians 7:14).

ACCENTUATE THE POSITIVE

The most debilitating force against anyone of us is not the devil and his evil cohorts who put us down; our greatest enemy lies within us in negative feelings blown out of proportion.

A defeated and pessimistic feeling is as real as a broken leg, much harder and slower to heal. If left to grow into a full-blown attitude, pessimism will debilitate faster than friends and even God can help us rebuild. An extreme awareness of our imperfections, those of our peers and our environment can deal us a very negative and helpless feeling. Many promising relationships go down the drain because we cannot see beyond the negative in others' lives. Some give up on themselves because they can't deal with criticism and their own sense of personal inadequacy.

A letter from Paul to the Philippians' Church (and to us) encourages a healthy focus, "And now brothers, as I close this letter, let me say this one more thing. Fix your thoughts on what is true and good and right. Think about things that are pure and lovely, and dwell on the fine, good things in others. Think about all you can praise God for and be glad about." (Philippians 4:8 LNT).

Applying Good Maintenance to Religious Life

I heard a foolish man say, "My wife takes care of my religion for me." In saying this, he revealed how little he knows about the very essence of the Christian life. No one can experience the new birth, accept Christian discipline and maintain our relationship with God for us. Others can pray for and help us but can no more save and keep us strong than they can eat, drink or sleep in our stead.

Jesus said, "I am the vine, you are the branches...he that abides in me will bear much fruit..." As a healthy vine or tree will bear fruit through its branches, so will the Christ bear abundantly through those who continually cling to Him. (John 15). All church problems, all failing ministries and all weak Christian living can be traced to an interruption of the "Vine-branch union;" they have not applied the simple principles of good maintenance to religious living. If they would conduct their personal and business life in such a manner, they would continually bounce checks, get their utilities turned off and run out of gas on the roads.

Our religious life is fundamental to all else and it calls for good attention which we alone can ultimately give. The church attending, praying, Bible reading, witnessing, disciplined Christians will live joyously, victoriously and abundantly—they will be lights to us all and credit to God's kingdom.

CALLED TO INCONVENIENCE

There is no accomplishment which does not exact a cost. Jesus said, "...Except a grain of wheat falls into the ground and dies, it will abide alone but if it dies, it will bring forth much fruit." Christianity is founded and maintained on the principle of Jesus dying so that life might come to us.

Jesus condescended from Divinity to humanity and to the position of a sinner in order to deal with our sinfulness. All Christians are admonished to "Let this mind be in you which was in Christ." (Philippians 2:4-9). While Christ's death carries a substitutionary atoning quality, our suffering is merely an inconvenience, something "which goes with the territory." Had Paul not been subjected to prison, we probably would not have these wonderful letters which he wrote to the young churches.

Christianity is a rescue endeavor; we have been called to participate! Our task is to help apply the benefits of Christ's sacrifice; this is the unfinished work of Christ. With this task goes unavoidable inconvenience and sacrifice. Paul said, "...I rejoice in the midst of my sufferings on your behalf...in my own person I am making up whatever is still lacking and remains to be completed of Christ's afflictions, for the sake of His body which is the church." (Colossians 1:24).

Continuing In Commitment

One of the greatest human faults is our lack of continuity. The world is full of things which are abandoned half-done; we leave a trail of waste and heartbreak as we go. New religious jargon includes statements as, "I don't feel led; God is leading me in another direction now." This may sometimes be true but can often be due to boredom, lack of human compliments or loss of interest.

New, easier words have entered religious language, which gives us a way out; they have replaced the old sacrificial words, such as commitment, endure, suffer, sacrifice, dying to self. Jesus said, "He who puts his hand to the plow and looks back is not fit for the kingdom of God." Like Simon who helped Jesus carry the cross to the place of suffering, we are called on to carry the information and benefits to the places of need. Those who enlist in His service to others experience this promise He made: "...I will be with you always..." (Matthew 28:15-20).

While on the cross, those who loved Him and those who hated Him called out, "COME DOWN, COME DOWN." The fact that He stayed until He could say, "IT IS FINISHED," should inspire us to endure and finish what we have been given to do. He who is "the same yesterday, today and forever" must long for us to also be predictable and steady.

DECLARATION OF DEPENDENCE ON GOD

On June 12, 1775, one year before the Declaration of Independence was written, the Constitutional Congress issued what has come to be called a "Declaration of Dependence upon God." The document reads in part, "This Congress—does earnestly recommend that Thursday, the twentieth day of July next, be observed by the inhabitants of all the English Colonies on this continent as a day of public humiliation, fasting and prayer; that we may with united hearts and voices, unfeignedly confess and deplore our many sins and offer up our joint supplications to the all-wise, omnipotent and merciful disposer of all events, humbly beseeching Him to forgive our iniquities and remove our present calamities."

It is a reasonable assumption that because of this Declaration of Dependence, God's favor moved upon the hearts of the brave men of that day, producing the great Declaration of Independence. Perhaps our historic past can teach us lessons for our present time.

Let us once more acknowledge and declare our dependence on God. He speaks, "If my people who are called by my name will humble themselves and pray and seek my face and turn from their wicked ways, then I will hear from heaven and will forgive their sins and heal their land." (2 Chronicles 7:14).

FRIENDLY FIRE

"Friendly fire" seems a poor choice of words to speak of wounds and death in battle caused by our own side. How very hard it is to find words innocent and tame enough to speak of this kind of tragedy. Maybe stupid fire, negligent, careless or accidental fire would be more descriptive of the facts which cost someone's health or life.

The tragedy intensifies when the injury is intentional. Those whom we are closest to and who know most about us can hurt us most and vice versa. Some of the fiercest battles are fought by people who once pledged their love and consummated it with unrestrained intimacy.

The Bible admonishes: "Stop being bitter and angry and mad at others. Don't yell at one another or curse each other or even be rude. Instead, be kind and merciful and forgive others, just as God forgave you because of Christ." (Ephesians 4:31-32 LNT).

When we are good and kind to each other, we are creating a good place for ourselves. The evil within, which taints our character with irresponsible attitudes and conduct toward others, destroys reputation, happiness and the high qualities of life. It is like a two-edged sword; it hurts both the one assaulted and also the one who wields it.

God's Laws Are Good, Reasonable and Just

The Ten Commandments were given by God to Israel while in route to the Promised Land. It is God's permanent moral code; the morality expressed in the Ten Commandments is applicable to all, in every age.

Our American legal system is an attempt to implement this reasonable restraint and respect system into our varied society. These rules are not right only because God wrote them on tables of stone, but God gave them to us because they are right, reasonable, fair and good for all of us, always.

The first four address our responsibility to God and the last six tell us how to treat our fellow humans. In obeying these, we will also be good to ourselves. They are: 1) Thou shalt have no other gods. 2) Thou shalt not make unto thee any graven images. 3) Thou shalt not take the name of the Lord thy God in vain. 4) Remember the Sabbath day, to keep it holy. 5) Honor thy father and thy mother... 6) Thou shalt not kill. 7) Thou shalt not commit adultery. 8) Thou shalt not steal. 9) Thou shalt not bear false witness (lie). 10) Thou shalt not covet (what belongs to thy neighbor). The Bible further elaborates on, defines and applies the full meaning of the rules for living. The Holy Spirit also writes these in fine detail on the tables of every heart in which He dwells and gives courage, power and the will to obey! (Hebrews 10:16).

Man's Last Refuge from God

Lifeless religion is man's last refuge from God. There is in Rio, Brazil, a huge statue of Christ who stands tall on a high mountain. Lit up at night, "CHRIST, THE REDEEMER" with outstretched arms to the millions below is an awesome sight. When I was there, the souvenir shop was buzzing with people collecting trinkets as were the grounds where they measured the huge shrine with their eyes. Sad to say, the small chapel at the base had no one in it.

Frequently, the most holy and sacred things of God fail to interest us in God, Himself. Many of Christ's followers were attracted to Him for the loaves and fish He fed. Judas was attracted to the money possibilities which the kingdom offered. As it was said of the sons of Eli who had grown up in the priestly environment, it can be said of many, "He, she, does not know the Lord."

In His last recorded prayer, Jesus said, "And this is life eternal, that they might know thee, the only true God and Jesus Christ, whom thou hast sent." New Testament religion is about the life of God in the soul! If in all our religiosity, we do not live in Spiritual intimacy with God, we will remain deficient of His joy, His power, His victory and His security.

MIRACLES ARE FEW

No doubt God can, and does, perform miracles; but those who count on miracles to always bail them out of normal life experiences will find them in short supply. Tornadoes plow through churches, as well as less noble buildings, and saints sometimes suffer great losses. The "get-rich" formulas preached by money-minded "pulpiteers" work well for those who open God's mail, but the honest and practical Christian will usually have to settle for "earning his bread by the sweat of his brow" alongside the sinners.

So then, why bother with being religious? Although our present benefits are called an earnest (small percentage) of our eternal inheritance, that earnest is far greater than all else on earth. Christianity sets us free from our past mistakes and reunites us with God. Those who are properly related to God can cope, endure, love, and all else involved in succeeding with living—they are said to be "more than conquerors."

Christianity is not God doing everything for us; but our being returned unto the full human God first made. Fewer miracles are necessary to bail us out when we live in His will. The Christian is at peace because he knows that when this life is over, it will just be truly beginning in eternity with God.

MEMORIAL DAY IS SACRED

Our Memorial Day Celebration is a small gesture in recognition of those who gave so much for us. Shame on us if we let the day pass without a deep conscious appreciation. Only by fully understanding our freedom, can we begin to appreciate the sacrifices made by those who paid its cost.

We, the living, should personally make calls; send notes, visit casualty families and gravesites. Silent appreciation is too much like no appreciation to do any good. Our institutions and churches must make a strong statement and all of us must guard against having a memory with no feelings. What a contrast those jewels of our generations are to those creeps who burn the American Flag to make a statement against something they don't like. It is good for them that their own freedom doesn't depend on their own ability to keep it. Could we count on them in a national emergency; I believe their conduct answers that.

Our nation is distinguished among nations in that we seem to have been chosen by Providence to stand in the gap between those who abuse and those who are abused. Let us pray that The Father of us all will always be able to depend on us for being on His side! In this coming Memorial Day Celebration, let us make it less fun and more contemplative, appreciative and prayerful.

LET US PAY UP OUR "THANK YOU DEBT" AND STAY CURRENT

The word "THANKS", or some forms of it, holds great prominence in the Bible. It is mentioned almost 100 times. This fact should make us want to express it many times, everyday! Our daily interaction with others and our God consciousness should call up a hardy "THANK YOU" many times to others and to Our Father, Daily.

The early settlers of our country, having endured a hard first winter with great hardships and loss of life, gathered to thank God for His supply of grace! "Thanks to God who always causes us to triumph in Christ!" The most moving example for us to savor is that of Jesus, breaking bread and pouring drink, giving thanks for the first communion service. If He, the one sacrificed, could say "THANKS", how much more we, the recipients of such grace, should run over with gratitude. There is deep basic defect with anyone who can coexist with others and seldom or never find reason to say, "Thank you" and mean it. In Romans Chapter 1, Paul points out how the Gentiles who once knew God fell into an awesome state of sin. He lists seven steps of departure from God and being "Not Thankful" is near the top of the process.

The Bible compares an unthankful attitude with the poison of a serpent. It destroys goals, wrecks relationships, and depletes valuable cooperative help and more. Let us repent of our not being openly thankful to God and our peers and to stay current! We will do others and especially ourselves a great favor!

Let Us Celebrate Our Labor with Joy

Our annual Labor Day Celebration honors work and those who expend effort and energy to provide necessary goods and services! The word "LABOR", by nature of its necessity, its provision and consumption, has attracted other words which spin off and broaden the Labor Subject. Some of these are Labor Union, Labor Party, Labor Markets, Labor Pains, Labor Relations and more.

Our Creator has put such diversity in His Creation that there is nothing lacking in all, which a normal culture needs. Let us all join the Labor Day Celebration with deep appreciation, gratitude and resolve to make our own contribution. We should be happy with what we have been given to do; we must develop and expend it. The Bible is filled with reference to Divine energy at work on our behalf: of Creation, its maintenance and adjustments, of Jesus having died, risen, advocating, preparing a place for us and soon to return, of the Holy Spirit convicting, filling, helping, the church monitored, developed, visited and kept.

The most important work and closest to the heart of God is forcefully stated in Matthew, Chapter 28: "...Go, teach all...baptizing...and lo, I am with you always..." Paul said that we are laborers together with God. As Simon helped Jesus carry His cross to the appointed place, we are privileged to help Him take the benefits of His Passion where they are needed: THIS IS THE UNFINISHED WORK OF CHRIST. (Mathew 28:18-20).

I Owe You a Debt and I Must Pay It

Shakespeare said, "The quality of mercy is not strained; it dripeth as gentle rain from heaven upon the place beneath. It is twice blest; it blesseth him that gives and him that takes." Surely, the highest quality of human life is a state of full awareness, the ability and dedication to deal with their own problems and also to help others with their genuine needs. They do not need to be appreciated nor reciprocated.

When Paul contemplated human suffering and lostness, he announced, "I am a debtor both to the Greeks and to the Barbarians; both to the wise and to the unwise. So, as much as in me is, I am ready to preach the gospel to you that are at Rome also..." (Romans 1:14-18). The Christian who has not yet grasped the heart of God, feeling as He does about other humans is regularly announcing that he is not yet fully converted.

May our love for others drive us to the limit in informing and warning them of the tragedy of lostness and the availability of Salvation. Jesus is so united with humanity that what we do to and for one another, He says we actually do to and for Him. He said, "I was hungry and naked and in prison and you did (or did not) feed, clothe, or visit me. If I speak in the tongues of men and of angels, but have not love, I am only a noisy gong or a clanging cymbal." Average souls are reaching for what they can get—responsible and spiritual souls are reaching out to all they can help. (1 Corinthians 13:1-13).

GOD BLESS AMERICA—LAND THAT WE LOVE

The name of our beautiful land, America, begins and ends with the first letter of our English Alphabet. The letter A is our grading letter for excellence in our schools. In world affairs, living standard, opportunities and freedom, it remains AA (double A).

September 11 (9/11) translates to 911, which is our national emergency call number. We called to God; He received our call and is helping us. America's position is to protect, help and fight against the oppression of smaller and weaker nations. We are resolved to rout the terrorists. There is not another like America; America is great, generous and helpful because this is in God's nature, and we have asked Him to help us be what He wants us to be.

America is not only a big piece of earth and water with a roof of sky and clouds, sun and moon, stars and buildings and roads; it is people, you and me; we are all part of this lovely country! Let us enjoy the benefits it affords and also take responsibility to contribute in every way we can to keep it In GOD'S Will—strong and growing in every good way. Every morning, let us ask our heavenly Father, "What can I do today for our great country and its people?" I believe He will tell us in a variety of ways, "PRAY FOR IT, LOVE IT, WORK FOR IT, ENJOY IT". It is said that one of our Founding Fathers said, "If you allow this country to lose the qualities we have suffered so much to accomplish, we will come back and haunt you." (2 Chronicles 7:14).

Forgive Quickly and Forget Promptly

The price we have to pay for friendship and all human inter-relationships is that we sometimes hurt each other. While some of the hurt may be real, much of it should be shrugged off immediately and charged to circumstances and conditions not worthy of clouding our emotions and soiling our souls.

We would be much more forgiving, if we could see how we hurt others as clearly as we sense abuse against ourselves. Those who hurt others need our sympathy not our anger— they are saying, in the wrong way, "I need you, help me; I am mixed up; I'm out of control; I am not in charge of my life." Carrying grudges weakens the mind and clouds the emotions, causing us to snap at the wrong people, at the wrong time and in the wrong place. Unforgiveness keeps our bodies poised in defensive or offensive modes, overcharging our system with adrenaline flow and playing havoc with our health, our soul and our relationships.

Our Lord said, about those who were crucifying Him, "Father forgive them, they don't know what they are doing." The prayer "forgive our debts as we forgive our debtors" limits our being forgiven to our forgiving others. We would do ourselves a great favor if we would release all offenders, even if they don't ask for it! Forgiving and forgetting travel together; the mind may remember but the hurt, the anger and the revenge will fade away. (1 Corinthians, Chapter 13).

Fool, Fools and Fools for Christ

April Fool's Day is observed by fooling people with tricks and jokes, which ignite laughter, mostly. Our Creator has put lots of laughter in us so we should laugh and if we do not laugh nor cry, we probably disappoint Him. "The young man who has not wept is a savage and the old man who will not laugh is a fool."

The word "fool" in its various forms holds great prominence in the Bible—more than 150 times. The rich farmer of Luke Chapter 1 had a bumper-crop which inspired him to store it and to gloat over his riches. However, God said to him, "Thou fool, this night thy soul shall be required of thee." He was temporarily endowed with earthly riches and was called a "fool" because he had made no acquisition of heavenly riches.

A most harsh rebuke, "they became fools" is directed to those who do not believe in God even though nature is full of evidence. They should believe in God by looking at themselves and their environment. (Romans, Chapter 2). Those who accept Christ's Salvation, live in kingdom discipline and enlist in the service of His church are called "FOOLS" but Paul quickly calls them "Fools For Christ". They are rich in what matters most on earth and when this life will be over they will live eternally in heaven's abundance!

Be Fair, Honest and Respectful

All human interactions have to function within a context of fairness, honesty and respect or serious trouble develops. The stronger the degree of abuse and the longer the practice of inequity continue, the more drastic the remedial means will be. It took a civil war to begin to remedy the injustice of one race, which enslaved another.

Abusive kingdoms last only as long as it takes to mobilize the energies of the abused. Justice and fairness are endowed with awesome power; they are God's built-in court, which rules over the delicate balance of peoples living side by side. The laws of our land are attempts to interpret and apply the principle of human dignity decreed by our Creator.

The selfish and crafty are eventually caught up with; equity and justice may be slower than evil but they are thorough and can be counted on to equalize. This principle of fairness, honesty and respect is at work closing and opening business doors, advancing and demoting in the workplace, making adjustments in marriages, the neighborhood and even the church. Six of the Ten Commandments and countless pages of the Bible tell us that we must be fair and honest and respect everyone. When we live by this rule, we smile, neighbors smile, and law enforcements smile. Our Father is proud of His family and "...He (Jesus) is not ashamed to call them (us) brethren..." (Hebrews 2:11).

A Well Planned Christmas

Christmas is about the longest journey and the greatest mission which brought the kingdom of heaven to earth. It is about a Father's search for His children who had lost their way. God had been working on our remedy for a long time, through the nation of Israel, the Old Testament, the Law, kings, prophets and common people.

Christmas is not an impulsive thought, an idea without foundation: "Who was foreordained before the foundation of the world, but was manifest in these last times for you..." (1 Peter 1:20-21). Christmas is serious business, well planned and coming at exactly the right time. Jesus' coming was like the payload which we send to other planets—a booster drives it, drops off, another booster takes over until the payload reaches its destination. God used many boosters (humans) to bring His love to our world.

Then, Jesus came; He was deity so He could help us, human so we could relate and know exactly how we feel. Jesus was assigned four Gospel writers with different viewpoints so that a complete account could be given of Him, leaving no doubt of the validity of Christ and His mission! Jesus said, "Fear not, little flock, it is the pleasure of the Father to give you the kingdom." May our main focus be on the gift which came from heaven to each of us and to fully appropriate this Greatest Gift in our lives!

A GOOD TIME FOR AN ATTITUDE ADJUSTMENT

"Create in me a clean heart, O God and renew a right spirit within me." King David prayed this prayer after the prophet Nathan confronted him about bad attitudes, which gave birth to severe sins in his life.

We know how easy it is to become contaminated and out of an unclean soul, an inappropriate spirit (attitude) adversely colors everything we say and do. In time, an ugly attitude develops a life of its own—hurting, maiming and destroying precious relationships while digging itself into a pit of social and moral disorder. The Bible instructs, "Keep thy heart with all diligence, for out of it are the issues of life." The quality of our attitude will determine how close or far we will be to family, friends, neighbors and our Creator.

Christianity is about helping us out of a quagmire of falleness and the maintenance of a clean heart and right attitude. Most Jews didn't receive Jesus; they expected a military leader who would free them from their external enemies. Jesus said that the real enemy is within. The religion, which Jesus brought down from heaven, is all about the heart being cleansed and maintained. If we cooperate with God, we can see the greatest and weakest sinner turned into the strongest and holiest saint. (Romans 12:1-3). The soul in which the Holy Spirit truly dwells will see our faulty, damaging attitudes replaced with love, joy, peace, patience, gentleness, goodness, faith, meekness and self-control. The Holy Spirit is saying, "Give me your bad attitudes and I will give you my good attitudes." (Galatians 5:16-20).

WE ARE SOCIAL CREATURES

We are social creatures; we are created with a need to belong, to be loved, protected and helped by others. These rank high—after our need for God, perhaps just under the need for air, water and food.

This social need calls for giving as well as receiving; it is a built-in tradeoff with very sensitive guidelines. This commonwealth access is a vast reservoir of knowledge and security systems which we cannot do without. NO MAN IS AN ISLAND UNTO HIMSELF. When we are down, it picks us up and when we are too high, it cuts us down. Some give up on their kind; they have an unrealistic view of how things ought to be; others are ill equipped to handle the frequent breakdowns in interrelationships. They are too sensitive about their own hurt and unaware of how they may hurt others.

The price we pay for the privilege of living together is that we sometimes hurt one another. Those who drop out pay a much greater price—they sacrifice helping and being helped. No one is so completely endowed that he needs no one. God said, "It is not good that man should be alone." By creating Adam and later Eve, God envisioned family, neighbors, church groups and nations of people helping people! (Genesis 2:18).

THY KINGDOM COME

Having been asked what might be the greatest discovery of the future, a noted scientist replied, "I believe that the greatest discovery of the future will be the inherent power vested in true religion." It is said that the heathen are mistaken in having too many gods and Christians err when we do not fully appreciate our one and only "True God."

Jesus' last words to His grieving disciples before His ascension were that the Father would send another comforter who would remain with them forever. In fact, He said that a measure of His own life would dwell in us. "He dwells with you, and shall be in you." (John 14:16-17). The Holy Spirit came with miraculous signs and wonders; thus was set the tone for the kingdom of God on earth (Acts 1-2). God would now be our God by a birth of His own nature within us (Hebrews 10:15-20).

The rule of God from within promised to give us victory in all circumstances, making us powerful witnesses and setting us in an offensive mode against evil. It is a duty, yes, and the privilege of every Christian to avail himself of the promised power of the Holy Spirit (Luke 11:9-13). If ye then, being evil, know how to give good gifts unto your children, how much more shall your heavenly Father give the Holy Spirit to them that ask Him? (Luke 11:13).

There Is a Good Kind of Addiction

I grew up in rural South Louisiana where the strongest addictive substances were Black Diamond Tobacco and Dark Roast Cajun Coffee. It is regrettable that, in the last few decades, we have been invaded with very harmful and addictive foreign drugs. There is so much money incentive in this commerce that hope of ridding our country of this plague is no longer taken seriously.

There is a kind of addiction which the Bible recommends in 1 Corinthians 16:15, "I beseech you, brethren, ye know the house of Stephanes...they have addicted themselves to the ministry of the saints." They were consecrated, devoted, and spending their lives helping and serving others. David said, "I have preached righteousness...I have not refrained my lips...I have not hid thy righteousness within my heart; I have declared thy faithfulness and thy salvation. (Psalms 40:9-10).

Many we meet everyday need our unrestrained Christian witness; those filled with the Holy Spirit and zeal will stay ready, look for and extend a strong witness! Their most fitting description is they are Christ-like! Before a foreign court, if we were tried for being zealous, passionate and witness driven (addicted) Christians, could we qualify for the honor of the verdict: "Guilty as charged?"

THERE ARE TWO OPTIONS ONLY

The whole Bible relates to and elaborates on this verse: "For God so loved the world that He gave His only begotten son that whosoever believes in Him should not perish but have eternal life." The Old Testament and the New both preach Christ; in the Old, He is preached in anticipation; the New, in fulfillment and application.

There are only two options for our eternal state; there is no modification of either. As we can understand the seriousness of a sickness by the doctor's prescription, so we can grasp the gravity of our condition by God's remedial measures. Perishing is so serious a problem that He employs drastic measures to save us from it. Everlasting life is such a prize He desires for us, He has committed all His resources to help us gain it. Those who don't accept God's help are on a losing course which is best called "Perish", an on-going agony.

The Bible story of Lazarus and the Rich Man is a graphic portrayal of those two eternal abodes. One did not go to hell because he was rich and the other to heaven for being poor—one accepted God's help, the other did not accept the help offered to all. The appointment of our eternal residence is at hand, nothing else is of lasting importance. (Romans 10:6-13).

THE POWER OF WORDS

All of God's creation communicates, but humans can relate in great detail. Words and phrases are powerful because they are the audible, if not tangible attitudes of those who speak. The Bible describes proper words as "Apples of Gold in Pitchers of Silver."

Words can ignite fires of passion, chills of fear and pit hope against despair. The Fed's Chairman, Alan Greenspan, says a few words, like his "Irrational Exuberance" statement and the market's stampede to adjust, moving billions of dollars from some accounts to others. God is always speaking to us by circumstance, conscience, the church and the Bible. His ministers are instructed to speak with the ability which He gives them and those who listen are greatly benefited.

The Bible is filled with words which give hope and assurance. They are supported by the wonderful words which Jesus spoke while on the cross—"IT IS FINISHED"! Those three words opened to us the kingdom of heaven with salvation and all blessed life! When we say, "I believe, I repent, I accept, I forgive, Yes, Lord," OUR FATHER responds with fitting words of acceptance and He is proud of us. (Ephesians 2:7).

The Love of Money Is the Root of All Evil

Money is a good and practical medium of exchange. The Bible does not say that money is the root of all evil, but "The love of money is the root of all evil." Those who merchandise harmful substances are not trying to hurt or kill people; it is just that their extreme love for money drives them at any cost to anyone.

The roots of evil motivation are always feeding in the soil of the love for money. We love money too much when we withhold God's tithe and our offerings, when we don't pay taxes due the government and when we see desperate needs and turn away when we could help. We love it too much when we do not fairly earn it, when we seek it by crafty means and when we over-charge or are not willing to pay true value for goods and services.

Loving money is not necessarily a trait of the rich. Some of the very poor love it intensely at a lower level of access. Our attitude about money speaks of our sense of values, of our state of honesty and of our relationship with God and our neighbors. There are a lot of ways to be rich, such as rich in honor, good name, good family, friends, happiness, health, right standing with God and our neighbors. It is a shame when we give up all of this just for money. (1 Timothy 6:10).

THE LOST COIN

The Bible uses figurative language to help us understand the tragedy of human lostness. "The ship wreck of life, weed-covered field, lost sheep, prodigal son" and one of the most explicit, "The Lost Piece of Silver." She frantically seeks until she finds it and calls her friend to share the good news!

It is very sad for anything of value to be lost. One's personal values can be lost in self-pity, addiction, lack of self-discipline or confidence, in rebellion or anger and like Adam and Eve, distracted from our Creator. THERE IS IN ALL OF US A VACANCY IN THE SHAPE OF GOD; NOTHING ELSE AND NO ONE ELSE CAN SATISFY THAT PLACE BUT HIM. All professional approaches to help the human spirit, soul and body must understand this or fail in their goals.

Our Father has the love and the means to find and rejoin the prodigal son or lost sheep to his family, to help clean the weed-covered garden of our life and to make our life enjoyable, valuable and productive. If Adam and Eve had responded positively to God's call instead of making excuses, what would our world be like? If we continue in our present direction and course of life, what will be the impact on us and on those we love? (Matthew 11:28-30).

THE HIGHEST CREDENTIAL ON EARTH

The Bible lists three levels of Christian life, "Babes, Carnal and Spiritual." (1 Corinthians 3:1-4). The Baby Christians are the newly converted who will need time and a good church environment to grow in the Faith. The Carnal have settled on the outer edges of Christian discipline and show little change in their attitude and lifestyle. The Spiritual, while not perfect, have attained a high degree of change. They are described as "having put on Christ" or "confirmed to the image of Christ" or "having the mind of Christ." They have a good blend of earthliness and heavenliness.

To be declared SPIRITUAL by the way we live is to have the highest credential available on earth. This high state of Christian living is not limited to or assured the church leaders nor is it beyond the reach of the laymen. The Holy Spirit, given free reign and cooperation, will rout all traits of our estrangement from God and bring us into Spiritual living. The Bible reading, praying, church attending, disciplined, witnessing, Spirit filled Christians will reach all goals our Father has set for them—they are blessed and their lives bless all others; they are Spiritual Christians.

THE FIRST QUESTION, THE FIRST ANSWER

The first question asked in recorded history was asked by God to the first creation, Adam. "Where are you, Adam?" He asked. The reply was, "I was afraid so I am hidden." Adam had experienced what God had said would occur: "If you disobey me, you will die."

The "death" was spiritual, the natural consequence of dependent creation separated from its source of life, like a limb separated from its parent tree. The first of many indications of spiritual death was the loss of security. This is a very scary place, without the conscious presence of God. Informed counselors have come to understand that "we are incurably religious," and we cannot be emotionally well if we are spiritually sick.

However, preachers of the gospel are saying it; the crux of their message is this: "God, your heavenly Father wants you to be reunited with Him." The words and phrases they use, such as "accept Christ, believe, repent, be baptized" are doorways through which they are trying to get us to pass. The ultimate goal is our reunion with God. Those who fail to reach that goal or again depart are still afraid and with good reason. The gospel (Good News) is that Christ opened the way and wants to help us all get back to our roots and more! (John 15:1-7). "I have come that you may have life..." (John 10:10).

The Art of Belonging

We are quick to recognize what belongs to us and we secure our ownership with bold legal claims or at least with loud pronouncements that, "These are mine, my business, my property, my life." A sure mark of a converted life is that one now sees himself or herself as belonging: First of all, we belong to God: "Know ye not that your body is the temple of the Holy Spirit...ye are not your own..." (1 Corinthians 6:19-20). We belong to each other, to the church, the family and the world.

There is no such thing as a private life for God's people. God breaks up the private life of His saints and makes it a thoroughfare for the world on the one hand and for Himself on the other. "...We are laborers together with God; ye are God's husbandry, ye are God's building..." (1 Corinthians 3-9). "...In whom all the building fitly framed together groweth unto a holy temple in the Lord; in whom ye also are builded together for a habitation of God through the Spirit." (Ephesians 2:21).

God will not let us rest until He has broken us for consumption by the needy. We are God's cultivated fields out of which He feeds the needy. We are God's gift to one another. The average souls are reaching out for what belongs to them; the spiritual Christians are trying to discover to whom they belong.

ROMANS CHAPTER 8
THE MISSING CHAPTER

Many years ago, I bought a New Testament of the Bible which did not have Romans chapter 8 in it. I have been an intense student of that chapter ever since. Romans chapter 1 points out the sins of the Gentiles; chapter 2, the sins of the Jews; and chapter 3, puts us all into one big human pile and announces, "There is none righteous, no not one." It also introduces "substitution" and "justification by faith" while chapter 4 further clarifies them and speaks of the harmony and progression from "Law to Grace." Chapter 5 explodes with the magnificence of "the religion Jesus brought down from heaven!" Chapter 6 is about a holy walk which the believers must adopt. Chapter 7 portrays the Christian's struggle with sin after salvation. If the Bible would end with chapter 7, it would leave us frustrated as Paul describes, "...O wretched man that I am, who shall deliver me from this body of death?"

However, the kingdom power for Christian living comes gushing out from the first verse of chapter 8: "There is now no condemnation to those who are in Christ Jesus who walk not after the flesh but after the Spirit." The chapter is filled with power, connection, reassurance and ends with no separation.

Attempting Christian living and ministry without the power of the promised Holy Spirit is like trying to run our car with the fuel tank filled with water, instead of gasoline. "...How much more shall your heavenly Father give the Holy Spirit to them that ask Him?" (John 14:16-27; Romans 14:17; Galatians 5:16-23; Luke 11:9-13).

POWER AND RESTRAINT

Restraint must be as deep as power or else one's power becomes another's tyranny. Wealth, influence and knowledge, not accompanied by restraint, can impose debilitating consequences on others. Our inbred tendency is to assert and flaunt ourselves over others.

So powerful is the inclination to take advantage and to promote self-interest that laws must constantly be revised and expanded to catch up with our resourcefulness in finding exceptions for ourselves. God's power is awesome but it is his restraint that stands out most. Those who would speak for Him can find all kinds of diseases, wars or natural disasters to attribute to His anger with His creation. Some, I believe, would turn up hell's thermostat if they could reach it without themselves being singed.

I feel sure that God would rather that those "sons of thunder" leave His name out of their impatient and vengeful babblings. If we could stop sinning long enough to contemplate God's attributes, we would discover and appreciate His patient restraint of the awesome judgments we deserve. He is holding off the consequences of our ways, while He does His very best to lead us to safety. God's nature and His church people get carried away and do terrible things. I may not, can not, will not blame God for forest fires, earth quakes, storms nor church people's sinful conduct. Eventually, not even God can keep us out of hell; that is how free He has made us. (Romans 1:28-32).

Motherhood Is Amazing in All Species of Life

The most famous mother in Christendom is Mary, the mother of Jesus. While we vary in our view of her present position, we all honor the mother of our Lord for her highest example and service in motherhood. When God chose to send us His greatest gift, our Savior, He sent Him by a mother who nurtured the Son of God to maturity.

There is nothing which we do in our careers and occupations which mothers have not already done. She is teacher, doctor, financier, counselor, carpenter, confessor, singer, preacher-priest, role model, chef, janitor and much more. Motherhood is amazing in all species of life and reaches its highest expression in humans. How moms nurture little babies from conception to productive adults is nothing less than a miracle in slow motion. Their God-given role is awesome and their trials are severe.

As I am writing this, I feel a strong urge to ask all of us to look for mothers who are struggling, who need encouragement, prayer, money, support, who may not know the Lord. We could honor our Lord and our own mothers best by reaching out to hurting mothers within our reach. Let us all give motherhood the love each needs and deserves. If your mother is too far away to visit, call her early! I WISH I COULD CALL MINE!

THE OLD RUGGED CROSS

Does our salvation hinge on Christ's life and passion? Did Jesus have to die for our sins to be forgiven or did He simply encounter predictable animosity in the process of trying to turn our hearts back to God? Is there reason for so many songs about the "Cross", so much preaching about the "Blood" and what the meaning of "Holy Communion" is? Are the church doctrines of "The Efficacy of the Blood and Substitution" relevant today?

Our whole justice system is a small reflection of God's greater dedication to justice. Every sin has to be balanced with punishment (compensated); either we let Christ's passion pay or we will face the consequences. The Old Testament blood sacrifices were designed to show the seriousness of sin and to hold off God's judgment against us. When Christ would come, His substitutionary sacrifice would adequately compensate and cover all our sins.

It is by the merit of Christ's passion that we have access to God. He said, "I am the way, the door and no one can come to the Father but by me." God laid on Him the iniquity of us all. He became sin for us! In turning to God, through Christ (by His merits), we receive our pardon and become as free from our confessed sins as if we had never sinned. "But the righteousness which is of faith speaketh on this wise...the word is nigh thee, even in thy mouth and in thy heart...that if thou shalt confess with thy mouth the Lord Jesus, and shalt believe in thine heart...thou shalt be saved...for whosoever shall call upon the name of the Lord shall be saved." (Romans 10:6-13).

THE DAY OF SMALL THINGS

I am your convert now, dear Lord, and I will make you proud of me! There is so much to do; I will by faith move these mountains for you! I lack not, said He, for those who will do big things for me. Remove the mote in your brother's eye that he may better see—go now I send you.

I said: Oh thou Great Healer, send me and I shall seek out the ill and heal them all and they will praise you!

He said: There are the healthy that are sicker yet than those you seek to heal for me. See that little fellow yonder, trembling with no one to give him hope—go I bid you, speak boldly, heal his spirit and restore his faith in me!

I said: Great Teacher, as the crowds came running to hear you, I would have you place me in a multitude and I will move them by the thousands for you!

He said: I have speakers well endowed but I need you to speak a special message for me. Go seek that solitary, lonely person; he needs a message, hasten on he awaits you.

I said: Dear Jesus, as David collected materials and Solomon built a house for you, I will raise the funds and build an edifice worthy of your name!

He said: No worldly building can contain my presence; go prepare the house of your heart—fill it with my love unfeigned. We cannot judge, we do not know which deed is small or large. All things large are made of many small things to which our Lord calls and this call is to us all: "Whatsoever your hands find to do, do with all your strength." (Ecclesiastes 9:10).

PROCRASTINATION
(THE ART OF PUTTING OFF)

A preacher of predestination, who got his words mixed up, announced that, "Procrastination is a fundamental belief of this church." Procrastination (putting off) is something fundamental about too many of us. The last few hours and minutes before tests or project completion are notoriously crammed with feverish catch-up activity. Sloppy work and product failures are frequently attributable to last minute haste.

At the base of all our putting off is selfishness; we really want to do what we like, what feels good and is easy. Regrettably, there is etched in my memory, valuable opportunities lost for no better reason than "later". Our temporariness strongly compels us to be attentive now to our responsibilities. WE ARE PASSING PEOPLE THROUGH A PASSING WORLD. Everywhere, God's Word and sound reasoning scream at us to break out of our comfort zone and seize the opportunities. These and more are small but important things to say and do, against which the clock is ticking: I am sorry, I understand, I love you, I appreciate, I am thinking about you, you look good, I forgive you, I am going to see you.

The Bible advises, "Today, when you hear His (God's) voice, do not harden your hearts." The place to commit is here, the time is now and the extent is total. The most foolish and disastrous words ever spoken are, "LATER, LORD". (Hebrews 3:8-15).

OVERFLOWING ABUNDANCE

The measure of God's provision for His people can best be described as "OVERFLOWING ABUNDANCE." The Bible says, "He is rich to all who call to Him" – "He can do exceeding abundantly above all we can think or ask" – "He gives peace which passes understanding" – "He saves to the uttermost" – "Our cups run over" – "We are made more than conquerors."

What are the conditions and qualifications to become recipients of such full grace? Can this grace be bought or earned? Is it for a privileged few? No, the value of sins forgiven, Christ in us and an entrance into His resurrection power which ultimately will usher us into the heavenly Prize cannot be earned or bought and is for all. Christ, the aggressor is pictured knocking at the door of every heart, saying, "Let me come in and I will make all things right and well." Failure to receive can only happen at our level as we fail to open to Him. He knocks at our heart's door by sermon, song, circumstance and never stops!

The religion designed in heaven by God, paid for on earth by Jesus and applied to us by the Holy Spirit, leaves no one out but we must say "Yes" to its call. The saddest day will be if we succeed in dulling our senses to His call or we are obliged to face Death before we have said "Yes" to Jesus. This would be the ultimate failure in life. CHRISTIANITY, fully received and applied is in "OVERFLOWING ABUNDANCE." (Romans 10:6-13; Revelations 3:20-22).

OUR SECURITY—ITS LIMITS

The Scriptures abound with assurance that Christianity is designed to save and keep us saved in this present world. No one will, at the end, be able to plead inadequate grace for his particular circumstances.

Some reason that our conversion is called a "New Birth" and that, once born, it is impossible to be unborn; that is, to ever again be unsaved, even if he curses God and goes back to the life style from which he was saved. They answer critics who point out obvious "backsliders" by saying they were never really saved or that their disobedience deprives them of blessings now but they will, in the end, be saved. There is another view that God, with book and pencil in hand, keeps flipping, writing, erasing and rewriting our names according to our daily conduct.

Well, the truth probably lies somewhere in between those two views. God doesn't remove the name of the repentant from His Book; He disciplines, corrects and He is patient. However, those who believe they can settle down with a diet of forbidden fruit and in the end, sweep through the pearly gates should consider the experience of Adam and Eve; if one should go back to the condemned place from which he was saved, to that same lifestyle Jesus said, "But he that shall endure unto the end, the same shall be saved". (Matthew 24:13). Paul warns, "...be not high-minded but fear...take heed lest He also spare not thee...continue in His goodness; otherwise thou also shall be cut off..." (Romans 11:18,22; John 15:6; James 5:19, 20).

New Time Religion

A church advertises: "Home of the Old Time Religion." Obviously, this church group believes that a state of deterioration exists in religion and they are dedicated keepers of important Christian values. They are to be commended for their devotion, but we must not overlook important changes in church thought and practice which are taking place.

To believe that old is good and new is bad is to overlook that the Epistles are basically corrective and teaching letters to the young churches, urging them to go on to maturity in spiritual life and mission. Christ's goal for His church is a church which clearly hears from Him, which neither goes ahead nor lags behind His truth and goals. He wants His church to function in His power, dedication, holiness, vision, and outreach and to have the "Mind of Christ" in all things, which pertain to heaven and earth. He wants His church to hold fast to the good things of the past while being selectively open to new and better methods and a clearer grasp of Bible Truths.

We must always be pressing toward the goal He has set before us. Such a church may well come to be known as: "Home of the New Time Religion." The Bible admonishes, "...let us go on (not back) to perfection." (Hebrews 6:1).

The word "Revival" suggests the regaining of positions and qualities once held and now diminished or lost. In religious language, it has come to mean the attaining of a high and effective dynamic in religious life. Some advocates of revival expect specific phenomena to occur, while others merely seek for God's full occupancy and leave the results to God's will and purpose.

Some Christians may be in a state of revival while others are in a cold state of life in the same church. Great revivals of the past have usually started with a few and rising in momentum until whole communities became deeply affected. Revival is the normal state of the church. It takes a living church to represent the living Christ; no dead body can carry a living head.

Christianity is all about life, abundant life, about God and His people in relationship, doing great and wonderful things on earth NOW! A revivalist of 100 years ago advises, "We believe that the voice of God to the Christian church of today is, TO YOUR KNEES! Tarry at my throne until you receive the gift of spiritual power; revivalistic, convincing, awakening, attractive saving power. I am waiting to bestow such power as soon as you get right before me and comply with the conditions of its bestowment". (2 Chronicles 7:14).

THE REVIVAL WE NEED (2 OF 4)

In our quest for revival, we are not attempting to lay hold on God's reluctance but on His willingness. God has never taken revival away from us; something has gone wrong with our receptivity. Revival is the normal state of the church.

It is said, "A revival is the result of concerted action, God and man participating, and when so promoted will win and last. A failure to comprehend the divine purpose so as to advance in harmony with the divine plan will result in disappointment. Every contribution to a successful revival on God's part is in waiting for the agreement of human cooperation. Gideon joined hands with God and promoted a revival by blowing a trumpet. Jesus, without assistance could have brought Lazarus from the grave but He would not. The stone must be rolled away by helping hands. God's word is effectual. His Spirit is present, His grace abounds. Let the church take her place, leaving God in His place and revival will be forthcoming—nothing can hinder."

Let us be sure that our motive is pure and that His presence among us is an active presence and then, leave the end-result to God. It is not too much to expect that which God has done in the past, to be repeated! (Ephesians 2:18-22).

THE REVIVAL WE NEED (3 OF 4)

The chief aim of all who seek revival should be the salvation of lost souls. This must be our obvious goal as is the Father's goal in Christ's mission to earth. (John 3:16). Paul struck the same keynote saying, "I cease not to warn sinners night and day with tears."

The greatest possible revival is one which would inspire every member to be a conscious, active and able soul winner. Forty-four percent of all Christians are led to Christ's saving grace by means of Friendship Evangelism. A single soul was audience enough for Jesus at the well and in the inquiry room of Nicodemus. In this revival approach, we can all be evangelists and one awakened church member doesn't have to wait for the whole church initiative to be in active revival.

In Christ's review of the seven churches, He appealed to the individual, "... who hears my voice and opens ..." (Revelation 3:20). The heaven and hell of the scriptures are not figurative; both are real places, the one to be saved to and the other to be saved from. A grasp of this fact in itself should make every day revivalists of all of us.

The Revival We Need (4 of 4)

Our yearly Thanksgiving has its origin in early settlement days when our ancestors saw reason to be thankful in very hard times. The poor of today are, by far, richer than the rich of those days. Money could not buy the advantages we have today because they did not exist. The early settlers had suffered told and untold misery but their focus was on the bright side and they designated a special day to assemble and show gratitude.

Paul traces our human trek downward from "knowing God, down to deep depravity." The words, "They were NOT THANKFUL" are listed near the top of their seven-step departure from God. Romans, Chapter 1 states, "A thankless child is as cruel as the poison of a serpent." An unthankful heart becomes breeding grounds for evil attitudes, which give birth to psychological, spiritual and social problems. If all we gave and received out of Thanksgiving is "turkey and the trimmings" we may well qualify for the name ourselves. We must regain the word THANKS in vocabulary and usage.

Revival, like water destined for dry parched soil, needs passage clear of obstructions. "Create in me a clean heart, O God, and renew a right spirit within me…" (Psalm 51; Philippians 4:1-9). May a renewed gratitude spread through the entirety of our lives and be expressed to one another and in our service to God. A thankful heart will provide good passage for the Holy Spirit of revival to travel from God through us and to the lost among us.

THE ULTIMATE POVERTY
THE ULTIMATE WEALTH

A very rich man observed a poor street boy as he pulled a green apple from a trash can and ate it. Referring to his severe ulcerated stomach, the rich man said, "I would give everything I have if I could do that!"

There are two kinds of poverty, both are very real. One has to do with supply, the other with consumption. Not being positioned to receive what is in abundance all around him, the poverty in the midst of plenty is the most tragic. Christ complained that although He and John came preaching in different styles, neither moved the hardened citizenry. A most pathetic and graphic scene in the Bible is that of Jesus sobbing over Jerusalem and uttering these words, "Eternal peace was within your reach and you turned it down. He wept, and now it is too late." They had positioned themselves beyond the reach of the love of God.

The poorest people are not those who have to struggle for the bare necessities of life but all rich and poor, who are rendered incapable of sensing God's invitation; they have not understood the Fatherhood of God. THIS IS THE ULTIMATE POVERTY—HAVING THE SALVATION CHRIST'S SUFFERING GIVES US IS THE ULTIMATE WEALTH. (Romans 10:6-13; Acts 2:37-40; John 3:15-17).

True Religion is all About a Connection

True religion is about a connection between God and man in which He clears our record and replaces our bad with His good and weaknesses with His strength. Christianity is designed to carry us rather than our carrying it.

Jesus said that the religion He brought down from heaven works on the same principle as a vine branch relationship; that as a branch bears the natural qualities and fruit of its parent plant, we would naturally and easily experience and exhibit godly qualities. (John, Chapter 15). Our responsibility is to stay connected to our life source. It is the continual and immediate flow from vine to branch which gives life and produces fruit. True religion is about the life of God coming to us; Paul said, "I live, yet not I, Christ lives in me."

In Adam, we developed a connection problem; Jesus came to reconnect us to our life source. Becoming saved and the Christian life are all about a connection! Jesus said, "Come unto me, all you who labor and are heavy laden and I will give you rest..." Our daily goal must be to live in continual spiritual intimacy with Christ. All religious services and observances are of value, if they enhance our union with Christ. (Romans 10:6-13; Acts 2:38-39; Galatians 5:16).

Unwrapping Our Christmas Gift

Little kids, especially little boys, can attack the wrappings of a Christmas gift with the zeal exceeded only by a hungry, mad dog. They are excited, curious and energetic and this seems to be the time to expend all of it! Giving less valuable gifts to each other is a good gesture as a token of the first Christmas gift. However, they cannot replace or be compared to the Greatest Gift which the occasion celebrates.

Jesus came to bring to us the kingdom of heaven and, to fully appreciate its value, we must consider the other Great Events of Christendom which follow—His teachings, His death, and burial, resurrection, ascension, the Holy Spirit's coming and the Final Arrangements for the Saved. It is a shame and a great loss of opportunity if the Christmas occasion comes and goes and we have not begun to unwrap our Greatest Gift. The kingdom of heaven has now come to us and all who will accept Christ will be greatly changed and secured! The Salvation Jesus brought down from heaven is so thorough and complete the Bible simply calls it, "So Great Salvation" and "Saved to the Uttermost."

The value of the gift is open to all and the most joyous, holy and righteous among us have not exhausted its supply. Let us give back to Our Father an act of appreciation which Paul expressed, "I press toward the mark for the prize of the high calling of God in Christ Jesus ... when I will finally be all that Christ saved me for and wants me to be." (Philippians 3:7,12).

WHO KILLED JESUS?

It is no secret that the Jewish hierarchy perceived Jesus to be a threat to their religious system and pressured the Roman Court to condemn Him to death on a cross. While Jews and Gentiles alike shared in the awful scheme, the fact remains that no one took His life but He gave it, a ransom for all. Caiaphas, Judas, Pilate and the whole gamut of those suckered into the awful deal was merely incidental.

With predestined council, God purposed that He would once and for all pay man's sin debt; secure the keys to death, hell, and the grave, giving all a chance (an open door) to the good life He planned for us all! We can all rest assured that His life was not taken by clever men but given freely in our stead. God was in Christ paying our sin debt—innocence paying for guilt, right pleading with wrong. "...The Son of man came not to be ministered unto but to minister and gave His life a ransom for many." (Mark 10:45).

Leaving the grave behind, He stood straight and tall and with voice defiant and strong, announced to His followers, "BECAUSE I LIVE YOU SHALL LIVE ALSO!" After making such a complete provision at such an enormous cost, Isaiah expresses one fear, "Who has believed our report and to whom is he arm of the Lord revealed?"
(Romans 10:6-15; Acts 2:22-24, 39).

Good Conditions for Creativity

It has taken time but I have learned how and when I am at my very best. It is when I'm hurting and spent, when the flab of my mind and spirit is stripped and when the superficial foam of my life is blown off to the pure substance. I am deepest and most resourceful when disappointed, . disrupted and devastated. A certain sanity of a higher form evolves, like a second wind of the mind and soul.

A free soul is too frivolous, too independent and too self-conscious to think deep thoughts. A long string of easy success breeds shallow and sensual gratification, leaving us incapable of reaching deep into ourselves and coming forth with truly deep thinking and caring. In desperation, we tap our own deep inner resources and are driven to search out other humans and a God who wants and needs to help.

We need to have the image of ourselves frequently blown off and the silly trophies we have erected on the mantle of our minds smashed to pieces so that the bare heart of our true being can emerge, think and act objectively. Unencumbered, our pride, our independence and our self-image become an unholy trinity before whom we bow and sacrifice our creativity. "Before I was afflicted, I went astray..." (Psalm 119:67).

GOD BLESS OUR ENEMIES

Years ago, a policeman pulled me over and proceeded to write a ticket. I searched for an explanation or a way out but decided to face the truth gracefully. When he handed me the ticket, I reached for his hand and said, "Thank you, if it weren't for you guys, we'd go wild and hurt ourselves." He appeared stunned as if he had never been thanked for a ticket before.

Jesus said, "You will know the truth and the truth will set you free." There is no solution in error; only in a context of truth can we find meaningful answers. Thank God for friends but many aren't tough enough and we, honest enough to hear them. We should love the truth by whatever means it comes, even by mean people who envy and hate us. Like coral reefs that sift through tons of water and debris for little bits of nutrients, we should look for truth in insults and derogatory remarks. Cruel and heartless people, like those who abused and crucified Jesus can be counted on to jolt us, to make us think and take stock of the good or evil in us. We must love the truth regardless of how it is packaged. "Buy the truth and don't sell it." (Proverbs 23:23).

Oh no, I don't mean to promote meanness; Our Father wants us to speak truth in love. (Ephesians 4:15). However, He wants us to love the truth so much that we can see and love it regardless of how it is presented. Jesus said, "I am the way, the truth and the life; no man comes to the Father but by me." (John 14:6). A wonderful present and future is in place for all who act on this truth.

MERCY ON WHEELS

Kathy's getting around where we worship, work, walk and play is confined to a wheelchair which she powers with her two arms and hands. I have never heard her complain about her plight, nor do I ever remember seeing her without a smile.

She was at one of our grocery stores when a boy was being apprehended for stealing school supplies. She immediately pleaded with the management to let her try to handle the incident without involving the boy in a police setting. She took him home to his grandmother then arranged an "aluminum cans for money" job with local stores for him. Seeing the poor furnishings in the apartment, she appealed to her church members. Later, the former little thief was seen passing out free candy to the church members, candy which was made by the lady who pleaded for the life and soul of the boy.

The Bible says, "If any one among you wanders from the truth and someone brings him back, let him know that whoever brings back a sinner from the error of his way will save his soul from death and will cover a multitude of sins." We are most like our Lord when our SEEING A NEED and our HELPING are in GOOD COORDINATION. (James 5:18-20).

P.S. The last time I saw the boy, he was big and strong and doing responsible work in a "Grocery Store."

THE DAY AND PLACE, THE DEVIL CRIED

Someone reported that the devil was seen sitting on a stump and crying bitterly. When asked why he was crying, he replied: "I am no angel but those Christians are blaming me for all their sinning and I am just sick and tired of it." The little story has made the rounds and carries an important message. Some Christians have given much more credit to him than he deserves; evil is always present, can be very enticing and tempting but there is much more power working for good than for evil. The Bible gives notice of the enemy on three fronts: "The Devil, the World, the Flesh." The Bible formula for Christian living is simple and clear:

1. Surrender your life to God.

2. Resist the devil and he will flee from you. (James 4:7,9).

3. The world; we are not to love that part which is evil: lying, cheating, stealing, hurting others; but to live by Bible rules. (Galatians 5:14).

4. The flesh has reference to unbridled and free expression of nature's appetites without regard to whom it violates and in defiance of the Bible standard. The Bible prescribes, "Walk in the Spirit and you shall not fulfill the lust of the flesh." (Galatians 5:16).

Our Father has made ample provisions for each of us to be a strong and victorious Christian in our present environment. If we are not living our lives as prescribed by the Bible, we have only ourselves to blame; we cannot honestly say, "THE DEVIL MADE ME DO IT."

THE FIRST EASTER PARADE

The parade begins...as the first day of the week dawns. With the image of the bloody, bruised body, hanging limp on the cruel Roman cross, followers of Jesus set out for the cemetery. Still ringing in their ears were the unanswered questions: "My God, My God, why have you forsaken me?" How could He say, "Father, forgive them...?" What is the meaning of His dying words "It is finished" and the tearing of the Temple Veil from top to bottom?"

The best news this world has ever heard did not come from gilded board rooms where the rich and powerful meet— it was spoken by an angel sitting on a stone at Jesus' empty tomb to some frightened disciples, "HE IS NOT HERE, HE IS RISEN, GO TELL..." The first Easter parade was not a display of people dressed up in the latest fashions; it was a parade of anxious disciples now reassured, walking with Jesus and telling everyone what His resurrection could mean to them.

The parade of people, beautified by His salvation is still witnessing and JESUS IS ALWAYS WITH THEM! This is the unfinished work of Christ. Like Simon who helped Him carry His cross to the appointed place, we help Jesus carry the benefits of His passion to the places of need! (Matthew 28:1-20).

THE INTER—FAITH ATTITUDE

Religious attitude doesn't lend itself easily to review; nobody wants to tamper with this holy subject called religion. Consequently, we tend to stay where we came in, pounding on the old foundation and never completing the building. (Hebrews 6:1-3). Those Christians who are secure enough to experience inter-faith contact and discussion will have a better grasp of the whole subject of Christian life and doctrine.

We must all belong to a church, but we should also be interested in all others which are also part of God's kingdom. "...for he that is not against us is for us." Not all true doctrine and faith is neatly packaged under one denominational name to the exclusion of some truth in others. This is not to say that error does not exist, but the greatest possible error is to believe that we alone could have no error.

No matter how much we know, there will always be more important information for the inquisitive Christian. "And if any man thinks that he knoweth anything, he knoweth nothing yet as he ought to know." (1 Corinthians 8:2). We probably offend Our Father most when we refuse to acknowledge those whom He has declared to be our brothers and sisters. We must compare notes; we must be students and teachers to each other.

The Local Church Can Not Be Replaced

I sometimes talk with Christians who have lost interest in the local church. They say, "Why be part of a local congregation when the church is brought to us by radio and TV?" Others nurse wounds which they say were inflicted in the church; some have simply dropped out, with some discomfort.

Misunderstanding and injury is the price we sometimes pay for the privilege of being part of humanity and its institutions but the advantages far outweigh the bad. We are social creatures who need each other; "we are laborers together with God." We are all advised: "If you find the perfect church, don't you join it—you'll spoil it." The local church is as important to the Christian as the home is to the family. The TV, radio and mail ministries, though very important, will not be enough. The local church is best prepared to develop the membership and to fine tune its function in the world. We don't abandon our home when a hotel and restaurant build next door.

The Christian must view his church as a commonwealth where he contributes and receives, a family in which he is an important member and a place which he must support with his time, energies, prayers, presence and finances. We must appreciate all of our Father's ministries and contribute in every way we can to as many as we can—yet, we are not to forsake our local church, nor neglect the assembling of ourselves together. (Hebrews 10:22-25).

Go To the Ant,
Thou Sluggard And Be Wise

I was working where 1,000,000,001 Fire Ants (estimate) had also staked a land claim. We were constantly locked in fierce territorial disputes in which I reacted to their firey bites with the speed and precision of a Black-Belted Karate Champ. They seemed to be reaching for the jugular vein and in route, left me bumped and pocked like an old Roman statue. I have called them names and in knee-jerk response have heard myself, calling to the Almighty to "save me from the ants, I'll take care of the elephants." Given time, I have come to appreciate something about the toothy little creatures. (Proverbs 6:6) In times of flood, they link their little bodies together, forming long bridges over which their brothers and sisters travel to safer ground. When the waters recede, many are dead, having given their lives to save the threatened.

Seeing this, I've been made to wonder, are we too individualistic. Have we become self-only oriented? Do we really care for others downstream from us? Evil has its origin in selfishness and it thrives in selfish living. Our Father must be pleased and proud of those who rise above selfish living and help Him answer the prayers of their neighbors, wherever they live.

The Bible account of "The Good Samaritan" teaches us that God needs our response to human needs outside the church, for more than our worshiping Him in the church. "We are Christ's hands and feet." "We are His appointed representatives on earth." (Luke 10:30-37).

The Most Important Question

Are you saved? The answer (Yes or No) to this question, determines whether one is successful or not in life. Beyond all doubts, the importance of our right-standing with God pales all other life concerns by comparison. The question evokes a whole variety of responses, such as: "I try to be good", "I am as good as most Christians", "I am religious in my own way", "I have time", "I hope so", and many others.

It is important to understand that heaven dispatched Jesus to bridge the estrangement gap between God and man. Only on the basis of His paying our sin-debt are we forgiven and the door of relationship with God is swung wide open. That is why we relate to Christ by confession and baptism. He and He alone is the "DOOR" and the "WAY" and no one comes to the Father but by Him. The good news is that He procured the opportunity for all to regain what our first parents lost through their disobedience.

Tremendous power is released in our lives when we turn to Christ for the ultimate remedy. With our cooperation, the Holy Spirit initiates a metamorphosis which transforms us from lost sinner to victorious Christian. Old former things are passed away and one is a New Creation in God's kingdom. There is every advantage and not one disadvantage in saying "Yes" to Jesus, now! (John 3:15-19; Acts 2:38; Romans 10:6-10).

THE NATURE OF OUR LOSTNESS

What is the nature of our lostness? How does it affect us and how do we find our way? Our problem is one of separation from our life source; we have lost our mooring and are drifting without our guide. We have become our own god and we live by harmful human values.

Abandoning God's rules for living, we have adopted ethics based on the situation—if it appeals to our appetites and self-interest, we do it. Being separated from God, we have lost our sense of balance; we live with exaggerated interests as mere caricatures of ourselves. Each generation finds new ways to refine its distorted values and to advance its lostness into greater depravity. While some of our peers may be more or less desperate sinners than we, all travel a common road toward destruction.

Our problem is not merely having eaten one fruit from the wrong tree; it is a departure from God's rule. Jesus came at great cost to Himself to save us from our departure from God, He sends His preachers to tell us all that if we will only ask Him, He will reposition us in proper relationship to our heavenly Father. Jesus says, "Come unto me, all ye that labor and are heavy laden and I will give you rest." (Romans 10:6-13).

THE PAYLOAD HAS LANDED

Let's not kid ourselves, there was a much more serious problem in the Garden of Eden than a couple sharing fruit under a tree. This is the Bible's way of telling us that we went our own way, leaving God out of our lives and living in selfish disobedience, "BUT GOD SO LOVED THE WORLD…"

A long term plan was put in motion to rescue all who want to be saved from the awful consequences of life outside of God's will and purpose. There is mentionable likeness between our sending space vehicles with payloads to faraway planets and the way Jesus came to us. Our planetary vehicles require multiple boosters (engines) which drive them toward their goal. One exhausts its capacity, drops off and another takes over until the payload lands on its targeted goal.

God's earthly focus was helped along by various individuals, families and holy people of the Bible. All contributed until heaven's payload, Jesus Christ, the Savior of all who will trust Him, arrived on earth, that first Christmas day!!! Christmas is about the longest journey and the Greatest mission. It is about a Savior, God in humanity, arriving with the answer we so badly need! Let us not let the "Christmas Message" be covered over by all the "Xmas things." (John 3:1).

THE POWER OF RECOMMENDATION

Advertising products is "big business" and those with reputation are sought out and paid great sums of money to promote and identify with a product. The Apostle Paul understood the power of recommendation and also of the negative effect of tacky Christian living on those who are looking for the good life. If Christianity fails to be attractive and recommending, it is at our level, when we are not empowered by its Spirit nor disciplined by its rules.

In Revelations 2 and 3, Jesus pleads and warns the Asian churches to recapture their first love, retain the truth, kick Satan out, reclaim morality, hold fast, let Christ in His own church. A survey reveals that 44% of all conversions were mostly influenced by individual Christians whose conversation, attitude, holy living and witness sold them on becoming Christians. The gospel preached is powerful, the gospel lived is more convincing. A sermon preached tells what God can do, a converted life shows what God is doing.

How are we advertising Christianity? Our Father has made every provision for us to be good examples, in every situation, every day; "we are laborers together with God." Paul pleads, in a letter to Titus and all Christians, "…That they may adorn the doctrine of God and Savior in all things…" Some lost people will read only the gospel which is lived out among them.

THE PREACHER, A TREE

Evangelical churches believe in the promotion of special services, "Revival Meetings," for the purpose of saving the lost. We attempt to create a climate of great spiritual intensity to show the unsaved their need for change and to assist and guide them in receiving Bible Salvation. Many of us need this special help, yet for each of us lies the possibility for this change by other means.

Surveys show that conversions are mostly influenced by "Friendship Evangelism" (friend helping friend). The most remarkable Salvation experience I have ever known of is that of a man who, on a cold wintry day, observed a tree stripped of all foliage and fruit; its limbs covered with ice. He reasoned that with the coming spring, life would appear and the tree would be in full foliage and production. He imagined that possibility also in his own miserable life, if he would position himself to receive life from God. There, he experienced the New Birth of Life; teaching us how very simply salvation can come to us.

We are conditioned to paying for, working toward or earning but salvation is a free gift obtained in a simple context of believing, repenting and asking. This opens the door to an on-rush of initiative from heaven to transform us from lost sinner to saved and victorious Christian. (Romans 10:6-11). THE EASIEST AND MOST REWARDING THING ONE WILL EVER DO IS TO "GET SAVED."

Why Only Happiness
When We Could Have Joy?

A millionaire 400 times over said, "It takes many things to make one happy and money is just one of those things." Some of those things are hard to keep in good supply and can be withdrawn quickly. We are happy according to the happenings we experience. We compensate with "happy-hours" designed to create a climate of positiveness and fun without harsh realities of our real world. We are happy as long as the happenings are favorable and unhappy when the happenings go wrong.

A higher quality of life called "JOY" is dispensed to Christians who "Walk in the Spirit." Biblical Joy doesn't depend on present conditions for its nourishment. It depends on giving the Holy Spirit full access to us at all times. No, the devout Christians are not exempt from the harsh realities of life. However, they are nourished by the Holy Spirit in a special way, as a branch is sustained by the tree to which it clings. Love, joy, peace, patience, kindness, goodness, faith, meekness and self-control are nine of the unfailing fruit of that relationship.

Jesus said, "I am come that they might have life and that, more abundantly." He saves us for heaven and also for earth! Very soon, we will discover that there aren't enough "good happenings" to keep us happy. Isn't it a tragedy when Christians are looking only for happiness when we could have a continuing life of JOY? (Galatians 5:16-25; John 10:10).

WHOSE BIRTHDAY IS IT?

A non-Christian businessman was asked, "Since you don't believe in Jesus, what do you do on Christmas day?" His reply, "Well, we sit around, counting the money His birthday helped make for us and we sing 'What a friend we have in Jesus.'"

I wonder how we would feel if at our birthday party, all our friends would exchange gifts, have fun and we were completely ignored as if we weren't present. Well, that is pretty close to what happens in many Christian families. What may have started as a good gesture, that since what we do for one another, we do for Christ, has lost much of the Christ consciousness? Yes, the season and the day carries a token trace of it but only the spiritually blind could fail to see that for the most part, Jesus and the whole precious occasion is not on our minds. We fall over with excitement over little gifts we give each other and leave unwrapped the precious gift of the first Christmas.

I am not on a holy crusade to undo tradition but I have purposed to gain and hold a proper focus throughout the season. I will give and perhaps receive gifts but I will endeavor to remember what the occasion is all about! "For God loves the world so much that He gave His only Son so that anyone who believes in Him shall not perish but have eternal life." (John 3:16-17). Christmas is about a rescue endeavor and the one who came to save us! Christmas is about, the longest journey, the greatest gift; let us not ignore Him at His own birthday party.

WHY DOES OUR FATHER FORBID LYING?

A friend walked up to me and said, "Alright, I have decided to tell you the truth." What he said shocked me and as soon as I could regain my composure, I reached for his hand and said, "Thank you for telling me the truth." Now I had the facts in hand and I could proceed realistically to settle the problem.

Only in accepting the truth about ourselves and our situations is there a chance to change and improve. Jesus said, "You will know the truth and the truth will make you free." This is not a new principle; it has always been good to hear and speak the truth. Lying and believing a lie, seriously corrupts, frustrates and violates. It is very tragic and sad that our legal system is tainted with lying and frequently, justice is smothered over with lies. There are no half truths, white lies or innocent excuses. "An excuse is a lie with a thin skin of truth over it."

For every lie that gives us an advantage, another person is disadvantaged by the same lie. The Bible instructs us to "Speak the truth in love". Love adds quality, like a cool drink with a bitter pill, when the truth hurts and calls for adjustments! Our Father who wants us to succeed, to be secure, well adjusted and fair, saw the problem of lying to be so damaging that He included it in the Ten Commandments along side "Thou shalt not kill."

Who Will You Believe?

"Because of His kindness you have been saved through trusting Christ and even trusting is not of yourselves, it also is a gift from God." (Ephesians 2:8-9 LNT). The greatest vocal declaration of an accomplished mission was Jesus' dying announcements, leaving us to ponder the question: "My God, My God, Why have you forsaken me?"—"It is finished!"

At the same time, by God's initiative, the Temple veil was rent from top to bottom, not bottom to top. Thus came to us the forceful, visual announcement that now we could go to our Father, personally, day or night, in or out of church; Sunday or Monday. We no longer need an appointed person to take our sins to God for us. God had announced an open door policy to all! We all need the salvation which our Father designed in heaven, Jesus paid for on earth and the Holy Spirit applies!

Matthew, Mark, Luke and John were assigned by God to give us their first-hand, eyewitness accounts so nothing of importance would be left unnoticed and unreported of the life, ministry and passion of Jesus! Who will we believe . . . the four Gospel writers or "modern-day would-be experts" who did not walk with Jesus then, nor know Him now?

WHERE IS YOUR TREASURE?

Jesus cautioned against setting our hearts in treasures on earth and advised seeking eternal values which are not so easily lost; those guarded by God and keyed to the enduring quality of His kingdom. He compared, "What will it profit a man if he gains the whole world and loses his own soul?"

In view of this, we should make all else subordinate to "laying up treasure in heaven" (a good record with God) our priority. The world is full of deteriorating treasures men have sold their souls to acquire; monuments to our ignorance of what is important. How can we tell where our treasure is? It monopolizes our thoughts, it commands our energies and demands our love; all else must give way.

If our priorities are right, we will always be better known for our Christian living than anything else. We value heaven's approval more than earthly applause and accumulation. These are Christ's words, "Lay not up for yourselves treasures upon earth…, but lay up for yourselves treasures in heaven where moth and rust doth not corrupt and where thieves do not break through nor steal." (Matthew 6:19-20). Those who, at death, do not have Christ's Salvation will be in ultimate poverty, a poverty vividly portrayed in the Bible story of Lazarus and the rich man. (Luke 16:19-21).

When Christians Fail, We Must Help

We accept progression with the inevitable slip, slide and stumble in all endeavors of life as being normal on our pathway to success. A coach knows that the ball will occasionally be "fumbled or thrown away" and a disoriented player may score for the opposing team.

We are awed by the unrealistic expectations some have about fellow Christians. We must be careful that our "Christian reaction" is helpful, restoring in quality and not adding to the damage of the sin committed. The Bible admonishes, "Don't sin but if you sin we have an advocate with the Father, Jesus..." (1John 2:1). "...If anyone fails, you who are spiritual, help restore such a one onto the right path, remembering that next time it might be one of you who is wrong." There is a remedial and healing quality built into Christianity. Perfection or maturity is the ideal state which we must always be striving for but we are not to give up when we fail.

If Judas had repented, instead of hanging himself, he would have been forgiven! Our Father's attempt to change us from rank sinner to holy saints is the most difficult project ever undertaken. However, there is no other endeavor on earth which is provided with so much readily available help. There is our commitment, the love of our Father, the Holy Spirit in us, the advocacy of Christ, the Bible, our church, caring Christians and more! Let us not give up on anyone, including ourselves, who are in the Christian process—GOD WILL NOT GIVE UP ON US!

THERE IS BEAUTY FOR ALL AGES

Our western culture has a fascination with beauty, especially youthful beauty. How to acquire and maintain it has opened a tremendous money market of information, materials and services. With fabrics, diets, lotions, paints and surgeries, we defy age's grip and lay claim to youthful properties.

On the other hand, we are almost oblivious to the beauty which accompanies all other age levels. "Mirror, mirror on the wall" cannot look deep enough to tell us "who is the fairest of them all." We should see the beauty of wisdom and knowledge, which age and experience have etched on the faces and character of those who have not dodged life's issues but have faced all of it, in good and bad times. Youthful beauty will continue to turn our heads, but perhaps we may eventually be mature enough to appreciate the beauty of all ages, including that which is below the surface of our skin. We should look for beauty of attitude, character, of integrity, experience, of friendship, endurance, of commitment, personal sovereignty and more.

The Bible speaks of the greatest beauty, "The Lord takes pleasure in His people; He will beautify the meek with salvation." Those who are experiencing God's ongoing salvation are enhanced by the personality traits of Jesus which the Holy Spirit produces in them! They are: "Love, Joy, Peace, Patience, Kindness, Goodness, Faith, Gentleness, Self-control, and much more." (Galatians 5:16-24).

THE RIGHT SIDE

At the battle of Jericho, a stranger near by was asked, "Are you on our side or on the enemy's side?" He answered, "Neither, I am captain of the Lord's host," meaning I am on God's side. A free society puts a heavy responsibility on us to choose. God and His blessings are always on the side of honesty, truth and fairness. Nothing can endure very long without these qualities for they must stand without practicality and His blessings.

We should be more concerned about what is right, not majority support or popularity, for there we will find God and His power to sustain us. We must resist other's personal ambitions and claims on our loyalty and seek the mind of God! The Bible says, "God blesses those people who refuse evil advice and won't follow sinners…The Lord protects everyone who follows Him." (Psalms, Chapter 1).

Right may be slower than evil because it doesn't take short cuts but those who hitch their energies to it will win because it is practical and God's power is committed to it. However, right loses power when the ingredients of intolerance and impatience are part of the mix. Right will make herself known to all who love and respect her, and the heavens are instructed to carry the blessings of God there!

LIFE AT ITS VERY BEST

Everyone must value and appreciate his or her individuality. Each should be grateful for the life given, regardless of race, gender and its qualities, whether perceived to be richly or poorly endowed. However, not even the most talented life is adequate alone; we are designed by God to function with others.

Our less than perfect lives need other viewpoints and the diverse variety of others. Those who fail to grasp this principle become inbred in their thinking and they lose practicality. Wisdom and strength are products of the multitude. The Bible calls the Christian community "a building made of fitly framed and lively stones in which God lives by His Spirit." (Ephesians 2:18-22, 4:16). The collective members called "The Body of Christ" function interdependently under Christ the Head and together carry out His great ideals while ministering strength and wisdom to each other.

Some Christians seem very close to God but are not close to other people. They have not understood their need of others and others' need of them. In saying, "It is not good for man to be alone," God intended family, friends, neighbors and religious connections for all of us. The Bible teaches that the highest form of life is individuality, blended and complemented by Deity and humanity. (Hebrews 10:24-25).

LET'S GO FISHING WITH JESUS

"And He said unto them, follow me and I will make you fishers of men. And they straightway left their nets and followed him." (Matthew 4:19-20). We will never be challenged to do anything as important as rescuing lost souls from their downward slide toward hell and helping them to become established in Christ's salvation.

Having been helped, we are all called upon to apply the remedial message at every opportunity. We must witness carefully and wisely or we could drive away more than we attract. "He who winneth souls is wise." We must be satisfied to be among those who sow the seed or water the plant while God gives the increase in proper time. It is a delicate process which can be easily over or under pressed but important enough to command our dedication to go as far as we can with each opportunity.

Jesus said, "All authority in heaven and on earth has been given to me. Go therefore and make disciples of all nations, baptizing them, teaching them..." Those who will engage in serious witnessing will soon discover that Jesus and His power are always present, helping them to succeed! How could we do less than to exploit every opportunity to rescue the lost and dying? The unfinished work of Christ is the application of the benefits of His passion where they are needed. To all who enlist, Jesus said, "Lo, I am with you always." (Matthew 28:15-20).

Lessons from Katrina and Rita

Now that we are returning from our days and weeks of sojourn in foreign lands, running from storms, we are prepared to talk about the ordeal. One biased guy suggested that we consider calling future windy storms "Himacane" instead of "Hericane", giving them boys' names; this might soften their blows and make them less spirited and more tame. He was reminded that there were bad boy hurricanes also. Others say that a warming trend caused by our fuel excesses is feeding the climate and we will see a continuing repetition of what we are experiencing and more. Still others speak of having insight in God's being sick and tired of our sinful ways and that He is ordering punishment on us.

Well, I am not prepared to give Him credit for this; however, whatever He does is right, but do you believe He would be tearing up His church buildings and throwing pine trees through the houses of His dedicated Christians who are promoting His kingdom on earth? All I know for sure is that terrible storms swept through here and generous help is responding.

An unusual sight is that of large trees, having been plucked from the ground are exposing the reason: They are deficient of large, strong roots and suggesting that above anything, in our marriage, family, job, community, religious life and all values—WE MUSTS DEVELOP A STRONG ANCHORAGE OR WE WILL FAIL AT LIVING. (Psalms Chapter 1: Read it, Contemplate it, Experience it!)

Jesus Announces the Eleventh Commandment

Jesus said, "A new commandment I give unto you, that ye love one another, as I have loved you, that ye also love one another." (John 13:34). This instruction is new only in degree. While He spoke this to His immediate disciples, the need for intense love, Christ's kind of love, extends to us and is to be directed to all others.

Most of us have some degree of love, but when self-interest is threatened; our love frequently vanishes as a morning fog before the hot sun. While being crucified, His love could say, "Father, forgive them, they know not what they do?" His love could make room for human pressures and depravity. His love understands insecurities and the power of self love. The degree and quality of love which Jesus wants us to have is very "patient and kind, never jealous or envious, never boastful or proud. It is never haughty or selfish or rude. His love does not demand its own way. It is not irritable or touchy. It does not hold grudges" (1 Corinthians, Chapter 13).

Christianity, fully received is designed to produce this quality of love in all of us! Can we imagine the power of the Christian and the church with this kind of love! This deep, intense, helpful and witnessing love is one of the nine fruit of the Holy Spirit the life of Jesus in us will produce if we cooperate with Him! (Galatians 5:22-25). He wants us all to "LOVE ONE ANOTHER AS I HAVE LOVED YOU, THAT YE ALSO LOVE ONE ANOTHER."

GIVE US THIS DAY OUR DAILY BREAD

God's blessings are measured in one day portions. We are taught to pray: "...Give us this day our daily bread..." The Bible instructs us to not be anxious about tomorrow; tomorrow will have the answers to its needs and problems. We need to concentrate our energies here and now. Coupled with this, we are promised that "As thy days are, so shall be thy strength."

The problem with being overly concerned about the future is that God's grace is released each day for this day's needs. When tomorrow becomes today, we can be assured that our help will be here. Should we, then, not make long range plans and be passive about the outcome of our projects? No, it is excessive concern, unreasonable anxiety and worry from which our Father wants to free us!

We are to be sure that what we are doing is in keeping with our Father's purposes and His way of doing things, then do our very best each day. We are to "trust as if all depends on God and work as if all depends on us." Such a partnership has all the necessary ingredients for success. (Matthew 6:24-34). "Worry is interest we pay on a debt we may never owe." Oh, God will supply the ingredients, but He expects you to do the baking for your daily bread.

Give an Account of Thy Stewardship

The end of the year is an important milestone in which we take and give an account of our finances to our government shortly after. If we are wise, we will take stock of how we have functioned in our family, neighborhood, church and all human relationships.

The poorest people are those who do not have Christ as Lord and who have not learned the value of human contributions. We are social creatures by nature; God said, "It is not good for man to be alone." We must be givers and receivers, graciously and constantly. Can we truly justify before God, the way we have spent our time, the use of our talents, our substance and our influence? Our life and all we are and have is God lent. He expects us to function at a high level of Christian life; generous, responsible and in harmony with Bible Christianity.

The Bible promotes the highest standard of responsible endeavors by placing our most common activities in a sphere of God consciousness. "Whether ye eat or drink or_____do all to the glory of God." (1Corinthians 10:31). There are calls by God to some works but other needs are defined as: "Whatever your hands find to do, do it with all your might." Some of the small things we do may catch the attention of Jesus, as Mary's devotion at His feet. It was severely rebuked by the money minded Judas but complimented by Jesus. (John 12:1-8). Be good to yourself, let Jesus into your life. He will forgive the mistakes of the past and help us succeed in the future.

DEAD FLIES IN THE OINTMENT

The Bible speaks of dead flies in the perfume, an otherwise delightful and exemplary life marred by problems. I don't know anyone who doesn't have at least one dead fly in the perfume of his or her life. The most beautiful flowers, as the best smelling perfume, create the greatest attraction, so the most aggressive, active and beautiful life can be the most vulnerable.

Things can go wrong because of who we are, where we are and among whom we live. Considering the fact that we were created to live in a garden, it should not surprise us that we are frequently strained and only the most naïve could be surprised when something goes wrong. If we could understand and accept the fact that life is a mixed bag of good and bad, much of our stress would leave us. For God to remove the possibility of hurt, sickness, enmity, death, He would have to deprive us life as He has given us.

Bible Christianity offers an indispensable contribution to life; those who grasp it are made "more than conquerors through Christ Jesus, our Lord." We cannot count on a problem-free life but we can accept Christ's invitation: "Come unto me and I will give you rest..." He specializes in the removal of dead flies which stink up our lives and grace to endure those which cannot be removed.

CHRISTIANITY PROVIDES LIVING POWER

A friend said to me, "I truly am a Christian in belief and appreciation but when I measure my life by the Scriptures, I wonder if I'm close enough to qualify for the name." It is quite easy to believe that our past sins are instantly forgiven but how do we avoid creating new sins?

Romans, Chapter 7 is filled with a description of the struggle to bring one's life into conformity with God's high standard of living. Chapter 8 holds the secret for victorious living. It begins with the announcements that those who walk in the power of the Holy Spirit will succeed and it ends with a declaration that nothing anywhere is able to separate us from God's helpful love. My friend knew about forgiving power but he had not been told about living power.

The most challenging verse in the Bible is: "Be ye perfect even as your Father who is in heaven is perfect." (Matthew 5:48). This is a high standard which Jesus has set for us and I don't know anyone who goes around bragging that he always measures up to it. However, this must be our goal. I am convinced that a made up mind to live obediently with a continual openness to all the help God sends our way will produce strong victorious Christian living! If we don't maintain our union with Christ and the Holy Spirit, we will fare no better than a limb which becomes severed from its parent tree. (John 15:1).

CHRISTIANITY OFFERS PERSONAL SOVEREIGNTY

There is a new kind of ugliness which is settling over our land. It is a new twist on the old word *hypocrisy*. We don't deny our bad conduct but deny responsibility for it—someone else is to blame; we are helpless victims of conditions beyond our control. Our expanding knowledge of the human mind and emotions has tilted us toward license to be selfish and self-willed instead of being self-controlled and disciplined.

Dangerous tempers, greed, and opportunism are everywhere in selfish expression on the road, the job, office. Some moms and dads are putting extramarital relationships ahead of family unity and security; all these and more speak of loss of control over our lives. We are losing personal sovereignty. The first goal of the Christian gospel is to place us in a saved state; that if we should die today, we are saved for heaven and from hell.

However, human life is too precious to waste and there are immediate benefits from our Salvation; we are saved for heaven later but also for our life on earth now. The religion Our Father designed in heaven, Jesus paid for on earth and the Holy Spirit applies, helps us to say "YES" and "NO" in all the right places; Christianity well applied and received gives us Personal Sovereignty! "Fear not, little flock; for it is your Father's good pleasure to give you the kingdom." (Luke 12:32).

A MOST WORTHY REQUEST

A disciple said to Jesus, "Lord, teach us to pray..." He seems to have asked about proper words and Jesus' reply is given in Matthew 6:5-13. Probably, the single, most critical and fundamental problem of modern day Christians is "Our Prayerlessness." When we don't pray, we are in fact saying, "I don't need you, Father; I can do it all by myself."

Will God punish us for not praying? He will not need to. The resulting self-deficiency will bring punishment enough: "Oh what peace we often forfeit; Oh what needless pain we bear. All because we do not carry everything to God in prayer." The "poor in spirit" who recognize their limitations are called BLESSED. They will pray and be helped!

Church attendance, good deeds, others praying for us are not enough. We alone can take responsibility for our intimacy with God in prayer. If we pray with the attitude and reverence of "The Lord's Model Prayer," we are assured an audience with God, Creator and sustainer of heaven and earth; we and our circumstances will have His attention!

A Hand Pointing Upward

I have been in love with a church building in Port Gibson, Mississippi, since I first saw it many years ago. It is a white building with a tall steeple on which a huge brazen hand points heavenward. Inside, among historic furnishings, is a portrait of its founding pastor Dr. Zebulon Butler and a plaque bearing the words: "He being dead, yet speaketh."

That tough, rugged gentleman of the gospel, with piercing eyes and telling face, carries a no-nonsense look about life. Bro. Zeb, no doubt, belongs to that breed of Godly men who call "a spade, a spade" and who could not tip-toe sermons around an audience while sin entrenches itself in the Holy Place. Inside, one senses he is walking with history—the pressing emotional subjects of the past, such as slavery, the civil war and women's suffrage burst upon the imaginative mind.

However, it is the hand pointing upward which speaks most to me. From all angles, it preaches this message: "There is a God in heaven who is doing His very best to help you out. The very least you could do is to listen to what He's saying." With blessings in hand, He waits and longs to get our attention! There is every advantage and not one disadvantage in saying, "YES" to Him, NOW. (Revelation, Chapters 1- 3). Thanks, First Presbyterian Church, for leaving the door unlocked.

A Fish Swallows a Preacher

A runaway preacher, a storm, they threw Jonah overboard, a fish grabs and swallows him and for three days and nights he is in the fish's belly. The fish spits him out on dry land and Jonah goes on to preach a great revival in the city of Nineveh! Just think about oxygen, enzyme and B.O. If you can believe that one, then nothing in the Bible will shock you! Well, Jesus believed it and likened His coming entombment to Jonah's ordeal. (Matthew 12:39-41).

It could really shock Jonah's generation if we could tell them that we made a capsule which was fired from earth, delivered two men to the moon; they picked up a few rocks and then brought them back safely. Of course, a whale doesn't have a throat large enough, nor could one survive in a fish for three days, as Neil and Buzz could not go to the moon and back in a mere tin can. The Bible says: "God prepared a fish..." for that aquatic lesson. (Jonah 1:17).

Thank God, He is not limited to natural laws or we'd be in BIG TROUBLE. He will need to bypass His own natural laws to resurrect and give us a new body when He will come for us! We need to know that His miraculous power is never far away. God allows pesky little problem fish to keep swallowing and spitting us out to teach us. It's a tragedy when we then shower, comb, straighten our clothes and head out in the same direction.

Why Stand Ye Gazing Into Heaven?

Having gained victory over death, hell and the grave, Jesus proceeded to witness His aliveness in person to many, by infallible proofs. He spoke to them of the kingdom of God for many days and then led His disciples to the mount called Olivet for His departure to heaven in full view of all. As He left, the disciples continued to look upward until two angels broke their gaze: "Which said, ye men of Galilee, why stand ye gazing up into heaven...?" The disciples returned to Jerusalem to await the advent of the promised Holy Spirit.

Jesus had said, "And I will pray the Father and He shall give you another Comforter that He may abide with you for ever... even the Spirit of truth whom the world cannot receive because it seeith Him not, neither knoweth Him ... He dwelleth with you and shall be in you. I will not leave you comfortless, I will come to you. At that day ye shall know that I am in my Father and ye in me and I in you." (John 14:15-20).

"Why stand ye gazing?" Paul said, "God has sent me to help His church and to tell His secret plan to you Gentiles...and this is the secret (mystery); That Christ in your hearts is your only hope of glory." (Colossians 1:25-27, LNT). The life or church which the gates of hell shall not prevail against is one in which the Holy Spirit is given room and great liberty to do His work. (Galatians 5:11-23; Acts, Chapters 1-2).

MAKING GOD LOOK BAD

I heard it again in a funeral service: "God needs this person in heaven so He took Him." As always, I cringe when I hear a well meaning person take liberty with God's reputation; to say what He has or has not done. No, I don't believe God takes little babies from mother's arms or moms and dads from little children "because He needs or wants them in heaven."

Life and death are left up to nature, to circumstances and prevailing conditions on earth. God can over-rule His established order in nature, but He must have good reason. On the contrary, we are admonished to take full precautions so that life may be long and at its best. Those who claim spiritual gifts or knowledge from God must strive for accuracy. We must all be careful with our Bible interpretation and our reference to its mysteries; we are far too presumptuous if we don't frequently say, "I don't know."

"….If any add to the words of prophecy of this book… God shall add to him the plagues written in this book; …and if any take away from the words of the book God shall take away his part out of the book of life…" (Revelation 22:18-19).

Who Is the Biggest Fool?

If we are interested in how and where we originated and are smart enough to believe the Bible record, we may satisfy our curiosity by reading the Genesis account. Some will look to fabrications, claiming scientific grounds like, "The pulsation of water gave life to a little piece of moss or something which began bumping onto rocks, chiseling little flaps which became arms, legs, feet and hands, after 10,000,000 years, crawled onto land, climbed a coconut tree, jumped down into a three piece suit and announced, I AM A MAN."

My faith in blind chance is not strong enough to believe that, even if given one or ten billion years. The ability of nature to adapt and repair itself gives us more reason to believe in the wisdom of a Creator and who else could He be but GOD—Who made us? After contemplating man, with his or her respiratory, circulatory, reproductive and nervous systems, brain and nature's balance and rhythm; reason must bow low and sing, "O Lord, my God, when I in awesome wonder, consider...My God, How Great Thou Art."

The Bible says, "For what can be known about God is plain to them. Ever since the creation of the world, God's invisible nature...has been clearly perceived in the things that have been made, so they are without excuse." (Romans 1:19-20). "The fool hath said in his heart, there is no God." (Psalms 14:1).

WE ARE ALL ON A JOURNEY OF CHANGE

We are on a journey of change—nobody remains the same. We are being molded by influences in and outside of ourselves. Every day, good and evil are set before us and we make our choices. No force or power can make us do anything we are not willing to do. We must take responsibility for what we are becoming.

It is very sad to see someone becoming afraid, discouraged, suspicious, bitter, vengeful, mean, and it is very refreshing to see others who are improving in similar circumstances. The Bible urges us to "Fix your thoughts on what is true and good and right..." Evil has not yet devised an approach which can corrupt a made-up mind but the unsettled mind and negotiable conscience will eventually give in.

True religion, the one Jesus brought down from heaven and uncompromised by us, gives much greater power than all corrupting influences in our environment. The Bible speaks, "...There is someone in your heart who is stronger than any evil teacher in this wicked world." CHOOSE GOOD, CHOOSE CHRIST AND YOU WILL SUCCEED WITH LIVING! (1John 4:4; John 14:16-18 LNT).

True Courage Is Like a Kite;
A Contrary Wind Raises It Higher

A lady said to me from her special chair in the isle, "If there is time, I would like to say a word of thanks to God." She said, "I want to thank God for this stroke which has left me fifty percent paralyzed. I am closer to the Lord now and my husband and I are closer. My self-life has been replaced by a more Holy Spirit inspired life. I minister more to others now and being weak, I ask for and receive God's greater strength." A moment passed and then applause broke out in the church!

Yes, a very strange witness which may be frowned on by some. No, we do not teach that God goes about striking bodies He made with paralysis; however, when losses occur and we are not restored, if we trust God, very special grace will come and be discovered, like new insights, values, relationships and closer walk with God!

We are truly a marvelous creation and in our present condition, there can be optimism, joy and new values to pursue. Had Paul never been imprisoned, we would not have his wonderfully inspired letters; he would have visited and not written to the churches. "Giving thanks always for all things unto God." (Ephesians 5:20). If we cannot thank God for our present circumstances, WE WILL THANK HIM IN THEM!

P.S. Thanks and enjoy your rest, Naomi Browning!

TO OUR OLDER MOMS: THE GRANDS, GREATS AND GREAT GREATS

What are grandmothers for you ask? Get me a pencil and pad, and I shall tell you why they live so long and keep track and visit now and then. I feel sorry for kids who don't have a grandma to talk to or to stay with or at least visit now and then. They are deprived who don't have a grandma to council and love them and give them a good setting straight from time to time.

They, like Mona Lisa who sits on the wall, can stare and be somber and shocked by what is going on. They blush and frown; they raise their eyebrows and wonder at the way these youngsters dress and waste and all that talk about sex. They grew up when times were hard and their mores were cast in hell-fire preaching on the ole campgrounds. They've worked hard to survive and they don't like change. Like Santa Claus, they can be generous but they don't like to see waste.

Everyone knows that they are loaded with antiques, jellies and money socked away, for they sure know how to save. They are the family tie which keeps us in touch with our past. They, like adhesive, hold young ones together and know what is going on. They pass the word around when one's luck is down or is sick or who's doing well and who is going astray. Yes, I know why God made grandmothers and why they live so long; it's because without them we'd go hungry, we'd forget our roots, we'd not get along and we'd go astray.

THE DIRECTION AND PROGRESS OF JESUS

Knowing that severe rejection, suffering and death awaited Him, Jesus proceeded toward Jerusalem on the day now known as Palm Sunday. Our Father had handed to us a religious plan which He had designed, to be released in stages, commonly known as "Law and Grace" and now recorded in the Old and New Testaments of the Bible.

The Law was called: "Our schoolmaster to bring us unto Christ that we might be justified by faith. But after that faith is come, no longer under a schoolmaster. For ye are all the children of God; by faith in Christ Jesus." (Galatians 3:24-26). The moral law of God is constant but the ceremonial and sacrificial were replaced by the coming of Jesus, the lamb of God. Jesus' teachings corrected much of the excesses and errors made not by God, but by men and corrections continue by the Holy Spirit.

Jesus taught us how to pray, to forgive, to work together. It seems that every generation needs its own Sermon on the Mount to realign doctrine and to put us on "God-Center" again. We must all be guards of the precious truths which define and maintain our salvation! May the progress of Jesus toward Jerusalem to give us His all inspire us to give Him our all.

THE PAPARAZZI AND US

Princess Diana's life and death, among others were hounded by the Paparazzi, photographers who earn money by taking and selling pictures of the rich and famous. They are well equipped with mobility, technology and an incentive which makes other endeavors seem to stand still by comparison. In an interview by an experienced news person, Michael Jackson, now among the most hunted by those merchants, begged for privacy with the fervency of a starving person for a piece of bread.

When the common person lists his or her assets, let them put down PRIVACY in bold letters. Maybe we do some of this to our neighbors in a less spectacular way, when we slander, lie about and enjoy cheapening others' lives in conversation and deed. We destroy happiness, reputation and a fair chance at life. When we speak about others, our remarks should have been subjected to this three point test:

1. Is it true?

2. Is it kind?

3. Is it necessary that I say this?

The commandment "Thou shall not kill" goes far beyond inflicting mortal wounds; it includes destroying reputation, good name, happiness and a chance to succeed. We have been put on earth to help each other. We are at our very worst when we hurt and at our very best when we help. Jesus said, "Blessed are the peacemakers for they shall be called the children of God." (Matthew 5:9).

THE CALL TO SAINTLY LIVING

Our Father's salvation is redemptive and also remedial in quality. If we receive only His pardon of our sins, then we have lost our guilt of past sins but kept our continuance in sin. Imputed righteousness, the goodness of Christ credited to us, has Biblical basis but our salvation is also designed to save us from our sinful ways.

The emphasis we must be hearing from the church is that the grace of God has come to save us from the past and for the future. God is in the business of developing saints from people just like us, who live and work in this present world. Their lives are brought into harmony with His, loving and feeling as He does about the issues at hand. Our salvation package includes the Holy Spirit (the life of Christ) coming into our life to help us! (John 14:16-27).

Gaining God's approval of the way we live is the highest credential on earth! The deeper we relate with God, the deeper we will openly relate with our fellow humans and their problems. Paul wrote, "To all that be in Rome, blessed of God, called to be Saints..." If all the Christians at Rome were called to that "high, holy, separated, dedicated, useful, enjoyable walk," surely the invitation includes us today also! Let us go for it! (Romans 1:7-8).

The Bible Is God's Book
of Standards

The Bible is the voice of God through the writings of men; it is the sacred repository (open storage place) of God's dealings with His creation, of His will, laws, warnings and promises to us. It is a "Living Word" through which God speaks to our present condition in all ages.

Our situation, our sin, righteousness, need, duty and future are spoken to in the Bible. It is God's official book of standards by which we judge and measure the validity of our own sins, attitudes and religious experiences. The Bible speaks of itself in these terms, "All Scripture is given by inspiration of God and is profitable for doctrine, for reproof, for correction, for instruction in righteousness that the man of God may be mature, thoroughly furnished unto all good works." (2 Timothy 3:16-17).

We must approach the Bible submissively, loving the truth and taking great care that the same Spirit which inspired it will help us interpret it correctly. The Bible teaches that the first Adam was created, did not evolve. (Genesis 1:26-31). The first couple on earth chose to live by their own reasoning rather than by the expressed will of God. "We were born in sin and shaped in iniquity." (Romans 3). We have developed more ways to sin than we have inherited, causing God to say, "All have sinned, there is none righteousness, no, not one..." BUT GOD SO LOVES THE WORLD. (John 3:16-18; Romans 10:6 -13; Acts, Chapters 1-2).

THE ABSOLUTELY NECESSARY INGREDIENT

Facing the trials, death and resurrection which signaled the end of His present, visible earthly ministry; Jesus told His disciples it was best that He leave, for a better arrangement would follow. (John 16:7). "He shall give you another comforter, that He may abide with you for ever. Even the Spirit of truth...ye know Him for He dwelleth with you and shall be in you. I will not leave you comfortless, I will come to you...He shall teach you all things..." (John 14:16-27).

Successful Christian living calls for our doing our best along with an additional power; a measure of Christ's life now called The Holy Spirit will come to us. He said, "I am with you and shall be in you." Our salvation experience includes Christ's life coming into us to help us do what we cannot do. The Holy Spirit in us will be reminder, empowerment, witness, heaven's quality Love, Joy, Peace, Patience, Kindness, Goodness, Faith, Gentleness, Self-control and more. (Galatians 5:16-25).

The Holy Spirit will add quality to our lives, witness and ministries and is the power which will resurrect us when Christ comes. (Romans 8:1-15). We need to keep the Holy Spirit comfortably seated and working in our lives, ministries, families, churches and all human activities. Jesus speaks to those who have not this power. (Luke 11:13).

Rising Above Pettiness

When we must get the most attention, the last word, the best seat, the most credit and when we rise and fall at others' approval or disapproval, we are petty. Petty behavior is everywhere—in the home, workplace, politics and wherever people meet. New Christians can be devastated by entrenched pettiness in the church. How much good could be done if we didn't care who gets credit or who will profit?

Jesus confronted showy giving, praying and fasting by saying that those who seek praise of their peers in these things would not get credit from heaven. He rebukes the opportunist who seeks to extract attention and advantage from every situation. He said He who sees motive and judges the intentions of the heart, prefers that our good deeds be made known only to Him: "Let not your left hand know what your right hand is doing."

Paul rebukes the nitpickers for meaningless details in religious life which have no input value: "For the kingdom of God is not (about) meat and drink but (about) righteousness, peace and joy in the Holy Spirit." True religion was handed to us in all purity and relevancy but it is at our level that it can become contaminated and made too hard or too easy. It seems that every generation needs its own "Sermon on the Mount" to cleanse, refocus and put us again on "GOD CENTER."

Penance Is Not Necessary

If a judge lets violations of law go unpunished, we call him "a crooked judge." Much more, the righteousness of God demands punishment for sins. When Jesus said, "It is finished" (accomplished) while on the cross, our sin debt was fully paid and ready to be claimed by each of us!

We will either accept Christ's substitutionary payment now or we will pay in hell for those sins which we have all committed.

The problem we seem to have with "justification by faith" is that it seems all too free and easy to be true. We do things for others; Christ's substitutionary death as a service for us is the same thing carried further and to more serious matters by Christ.

It is offensive to Christ when we repent of our sins and still feel we must do penance for them. By trying to further satisfy with payments of our own, we say in fact, "Christ's offer is not enough." Our confessed sins are "cast into the sea of forgetfulness, never to be remembered." However, the faith which saves must be serious enough to express it by repentance and baptism. Mistakes and sins of Christians are also forgiven as confessed and despised in our hearts. The critical issue is that sinning is a symptom of our estrangement from Our Father. Christ's mission is also to remedy the cause of sinning by bringing us close to God and His help He has arranged for us. Practices which add to or take away from Our Father's remedy will not save us. (Ephesians 2:4-9).

Life Is Like a Tree

I have purposed this Christmas to inquire into the sacred season for a deeper meaning or at least a dimension of the Holiday Subject I have not yet seen. I turned for inspiration to the Holy Writ, the worship, the carols, the market place, the media, and especially to the Holy Spirit.

Finally, I see it! A humble, obscure tree of the forest is brought into the most important room of the house and the whole family expends their talents to transform it into a Christmas tree. It is decorated and laden with gifts and honored to bear the Star of Christ on its bough. That lowly tree now becomes a meeting place around which love, joy, unity and gifts abound.

This is exactly what Christmas is all about. The lonely, the obscure, as well as all others, are sought out; their lives are trimmed and beautified to be enjoyed and for all to see and be blessed. Yes, Christmas means change for the better. The substance of the angelic message on that first Christmas morn is "The Christ has come to enhance and improve our lives. We must take Him seriously, we must submit to His approach. He changes us by beginning on the inside and very soon our whole life is secured, beautified, made valuable and saved for eternity!" (John 3:16-17). Have you unwrapped your first Christmas gift? He is most valuable!

Jesus Reviews His Churches

The first part of the book of Revelation is about Jesus' review of the seven churches of Asia. From these three chapters, we are to understand that He monitors His churches, keeps His own records and doesn't act by majority vote. His appearance was so overwhelming that John fell as dead before the awesome presence.

He is seen walking among seven candlesticks (churches) and announcing, "I know your works…" He commends where He sees good and forcefully rebukes wrong. To the Church of Ephesus, He says, "You have lost your first love, repent…" One church not reprimanded was going through tribulation and poverty. Another was told, "You have a little strength, I have left you an open door and no man can shut it". To Pergamos, He said, "I know where Satan's seat is…" Finally, to the Church of the Laodiceans, "You are neither cold nor hot. I will spue you out of my mouth." You say, "I am rich and increased with goods and have need of nothing…but I see you wretched, miserable, poor, blind and naked." He is pictured outside and appealing to the individuals to let Him in.

Our Lord made all needed provisions for His church to be strong, holy and helpful; when His church fails, the whole world suffers. Our Lord continues to review His churches; what could He be saying about our church, yours, about you and me? (Revelations, Chapters 1-3).

IF WE GO FOR HIM, HE WILL GO WITH US

I am endeavoring in this season of celebrating the crucifixion and resurrection of Christ to inquire more deeply in the holy subjects for impressions which might bring me into a more harmonious life with heavenly principles. I admire Mary and Joseph's dedication and submission, the enthusiastic angels who announced His birth, the shepherds who left all to be part of the sacred event and the wise men who traveled far and gave gifts to Jesus. Their witness was about a baby, a beginning of our Father's wonderful redemptive plan for us all.

We now have much more to report than they; we have the whole completed gospel (Good News) to proclaim. We can report about His death, burial, resurrection, ascension and the Holy Spirit who came to help us live the Christian life! We now have firsthand knowledge and experience of the grace of God at work in the human soul. We are all asked to join Joseph, Mary, the angels, the shepherds, the wise men, the Apostles, the Saints of past and present to be like His Star and lead others to Jesus.

Let us renew, refresh, increase and dedicate ourselves to the mission of HELPING JESUS APPLY THE BENEFITS OF HIS PASSION WHERE THEY ARE NEEDED. HE HAS PROMISED IF WE GO WIN SOULS FOR HIM, HE WILL GO WITH US. (Mathew 28:18-20).

THE NINE BEATITUDES OF JESUS, CONTEMPLATED

Do we want that quality of life which helps others, pleases our Father and enhances our own quality of life? Let us spend time understanding the meaning of the nine Beatitudes and the way of adopting them in our present life.

1. Blessed are the poor in spirit for theirs is the kingdom of heaven.

2. Blessed are they that mourn, for they shall be comforted.

3. Blessed are the meek, for they shall inherit the earth.

4. Blessed are they which do hunger and thirst after righteousness for they shall be filled.

5. Blessed are the merciful for they shall obtain mercy.

6. Blessed are the pure in heart for they shall see God.

7. Blessed are the peacemakers for they shall be called the Children of God.

8. Blessed are they which are persecuted for righteousness sake for theirs is the kingdom of heaven.

9. Blessed are ye, when men shall revile you, and persecute you, and shall say all manner of evil against you falsely, for my sake. Rejoice, and be exceeding glad; for great is your reward in heaven." (Matthew 5).

Jesus spoke these; let us study their meaning and apply them to our present life. To the extent that we grasp their meaning and apply those principles in daily living, we will be helpful to others, pleasing to God, live productively, joyously and successfully!

FINE TUNING AND REDEDICATING OUR LIVES

Some time ago, I became consciously inspired to begin an emphasis on "Fine Tuning" our Christian lives. A dear friend had confided, "I am not as close to God as I used to be." How regrettable that we may have lost ground once gained, when God is looking for progress and we need it.

Other ministers in the church caught the spirit of it and began to experience and promote the value of closeness to God. Conformity to our Father's will and His invitation to the deeper life became a theme with no holds barred and without condemnation toward anyone who may not go along. We added to the communion service an invitation to scriptural anointing and the laying on of hands by the elders for those with problems. Soon, members began asking for opportunity to share about healings of spirit, soul, body and relationships. Pesky church problems began to get fixed. Christian love flourished and began flowing to all and in all directions, attracting others to "victorious living".

We soon began to understand that we were locking into a divine principle: "Come close to God and He will come close to you..." (James 4:8-10; Revelation 3:20) "...Don't copy the behavior and customs of this world but be a new and different person with a fresh newness in all you do and think. Then you will learn from your own experience how His ways will really satisfy you." (Romans 12:1-2 LAT).

WHAT TYPE OF WORSHIP PLEASES OUR FATHER?

Our Creator (God) chose to create us in great variety. While there is great similarity, we are not completely like anyone else. We soon notice that new acquaintances are different not only in physical appearance but also in personality, temperament, actions, reactions, likes and dislikes. A compliment or a gift will cause one to jump, holler and in every way respond loudly, while another may react quietly; he or she sits and cries. Both express their honest feelings but they are designed to be different.

Knowledge of personal and social sciences has done very much to bring acceptance to individuals and our differences. Man made perimeters have loosened their tight grip on individualities to let us be who we really are. However, it is never right to sin against God's rules for living which He made for our own good; no one can say, "I am just made that way; I have to sin."

Some of us will naturally express ourselves more loudly and some more quietly in the same service which is designed to glorify God and to give Spiritual sustenance to the members of Christ's body, the church. The Bible and common sense call for sincerity and in being ourselves in personal worship and having respect for the established order in churches we attend and visit. The words, "Loud voices, of praise, of the trumpet and a quiet spirit and be still before our God" probably mean: "Give God your very best in the way you are designed to express yourself and to worship Him and don't despise another next to you for being quieter or louder than you."

CROSS CARRYING

I don't know anyone who doesn't have a problem, "a fly in the perfume of his life", or a cross to bear. Paul asked God three times to take away his "thorn in the flesh" but God said no, that sufficient grace would be provided to bear it. God always answers sincere prayer and if one cannot accept all of the possible answers, "yes, no, wait awhile", he should not waste his or God's time in prayer.

We will encounter hardships because of who we are, where we are, and among whom we live. There is our own inner cross, the cross of inter-personal conflicts, of gain and loss, of religious matters, and more. Jesus said, "If anyone takes hold of the plow and looks back, he is not fit for the kingdom." The application of the remedies for which Christ died will exact a toll on all who enlist for "The Great Commission." (Philippians 1:29).

Jesus said, "You cannot be my disciple..." unless you carry your own cross and come with me. You cannot come with me unless you love me more than you love your own life." (Luke 14:25-27). If we live, truly live this year, unavoidable crosses will be laid upon us. If we can't beg nor pray them off, we will be given grace to bear them.

We Must All Be Students and Teachers

It is natural that people of like views would bond together to express and promote their beliefs. Church denominations or fellowships have a generally agreed upon center of belief and practice. Individual members may have some different views, slightly left or right of the established middle ground. This does not mean that they are purposely in disagreement; this is what they understand now to be the truth. Those honest differences may strain the fellowships but the variations are not usually great enough to break them apart.

Even Christ's immediate followers had disagreements and personal conflicts and except for His intervention they might have splintered apart. It is the love, wisdom and tolerance of Jesus among us which continues to be the adhesive which binds people together. In an appeal for unity, Paul wrote, "Be humble and gentle; be patient with each other's faults; try always to be led along together by the Holy Spirit and to be at peace with one another; we are all parts of one future; there is only one Lord, one faith, one baptism; we all have the same God." (Ephesians 4:1-6 LNT).

The worst thing that could happen to a father is that his children would not love each other, would fight one another. THE WORST POSSIBLE ERROR IS TO BELIEVE THAT WE ALONE COULD HAVE NO ERROR.

WE ARE ALL PREACHERS

Normal Christianity is on the move in its neighborhood and is always pressing outward toward the "uttermost parts of the world." Those who would see it at its best will have to be involved in its outreach.

Christ's promise, "Lo I am with you always," was made in connection with His instructions to go to all nations to share the gospel. (Matthew 28:18-20). This bright light of truth is too important to be "put under a bushel"; it must be held high for all to clearly see. We've all been licensed and ordained by God to tell others what we know and have experienced. (John 15:16).

Those who say that their faith is a private matter between God and themselves and feel no inner urge to share its life giving message, show how shallow an entrance they have made into the deep things of God. Could we withhold information which is vital to another's health or safety? How much more we must alert all we see with Christ's remedial message. Most of what we will do today will be of temporary value. Nothing will be as important as having shared the love of God by word or deed! Yes, we are all preachers, promoting values; it's too bad that we spend so much time promoting temporary instead of eternal values.

TRACKING WITH JESUS—GRAVE TO HEAVEN

If you read and compare the four Gospels, you can quickly see the wisdom of having the version of each telling the same story with each its viewpoint. Jesus' life is too big and important for only one report. What is clear is that all who wanted to see Him were looking for Him and Jesus did all they needed to satisfy their thirst for proof.

Those who "SEEK, find Him; ASK, are given; KNOCK at His door, have access" that is, He has an open door relationship with all who want it. I recommend to all that we profitably spend one or two hours in reading the following verses: (Matthew 27-28; Mark 15-16; Luke 23-24; John 20-21; Acts 1-2). If your job pays you a thousand dollars per hour, you will receive far more values by getting a good grasp of the details of what Jesus did for you and all of us. There is no end to His generosity; the resulting Salvation which His passion paid for is so awesome, broad, and vast that the Bible simply calls it "So Great Salvation" and "Saved to the Uttermost."

"Go tell" are prominent words throughout the Bible. Last words are notoriously important at weddings, deaths, departures and especially Jesus' last words before going to heaven. Our Salvation can be "so great" because it includes a measure of His life coming into our life. May we all grasp the Holy Spirit message; this is part of our salvation package. (John, Chapters 14-15). Word from Him has reached us that He is in heaven and is about to come get us!!!

Total Honesty—Why Not?

"As he thinks in his heart, so is he." If we can see beyond pretense, past excuses and accommodating behavior, we will see the true person. What we say does not always reveal us; what we are speaks more loudly. A most memorable statement I heard was made by a little Catholic Nun. She said, "I am very careful not to give the impression that I am better than I am."

In this day of cover up, political correctness and openly ignoring God's instruction to always tell the truth, arriving at the truth about something or someone can be difficult and expensive; it is refreshing to see total honesty! Such an unpretentious attitude could be found only in someone who knows the value of truth, who understands the essentials of human interaction and takes God's word seriously. There are too few teachers and students of "Total Truth Living". It is regrettable that our adversary approach to justice focuses more on winning a case than the discovery of truth. Pretense thrives in our culture and at times even finds its way into the church.

The value of truth is highlighted in the Bible, "You shall know the truth and the truth shall make you free. Stop lying to each other; tell the truth, for we are parts of each other and when we lie to each other we are hurting ourselves also." (Ephesians 4:25 LNT).

To Everyone, A Cross

I don't know anyone who doesn't have problems; and, if I should see one, I would suggest that he helps others with their crosses. The complexity of our times imposes heavy burdens on us and most face up to them. Some attempt to shift theirs to another or even create problems for others, taking no responsibility for their conduct.

We may believe our cross is heaviest because we know it in greater detail; we cannot feel the pain of another. We function at a fraction of our capacity; there seems to always be more ability and flexibility to meet the new challenges. Frequently, we flourish in spirit, in social and religious life in the most severe trials because we grasp true values and God's grace in our desperation. We are at our very best when we see the needs around us and extend a helping hand; we are then most like our Lord.

As Simon assisted Jesus with His cross, He continues to need us to help with the burdens He carries because of and for us; we are His hands extended to help. Jesus said, "Unless you take up your cross and fellow me, ye cannot be my disciples." A Christian without a cross is not a completed Christian: Christian means Christ like and Christ carries a cross.

THE GREATEST TRUST AND ASSIGNMENT

A great amount of trust is placed on anyone who is part of a household, a community, church, public services, on the highways. The Bible announces THE GREATEST TRUST: "We were allowed of God to be put in trust with the gospel..." (1Thessalonians 2:4-13). His ministers must be responsible, passionate and accurate. The gospel is not information only but also accompanying power of the Holy Spirit to apply our Lord's remedy. (1Thessalonians 1:5).

All Christians are given the GREATEST ASSIGNMENT EVER GIVEN: "Go and make disciples in all the nations...and then teach these new disciples to obey all the commands...and be sure of this, that I am with you always..." (Matthew 28:19-20). A study reveals that 44% of all converts are won by our personal witness and example called "Friendship Evangelism".

It is dreadful to think that we may have driven away some by our uncaring, coldness and poor examples. This Bible message applies to all of us, "Remind Archippus to do the work that the Lord has given him to do." (Colossians 4:17). The unfinished work of Christ is the application of the benefits of His passion where they are needed. For every lost person, one of us is in the best position to reach him or her— TODAY would be the best day to begin!

THE BEST NEWS IS THE GOSPEL NEWS

The gospel is the information which comes to us about God's provision for our salvation! The provision is based on Jesus' death, burial and resurrection. It is not only information but accompanying power to bring change in all who will believe and ask.

The gospel is called, "The power of God unto salvation." This salvation is so thorough and extensive that it defies description. The Bible simply says, "Christ is rich to all who call on His name" and calls it "So Great Salvation, Saves To The Utmost." There is no question about who initiated our gospel or who paid the cost. (John 3:16-18). The Holy Spirit assists us from being lost to Salvation, to growth and maturing. The greatest assignment given to humans is "THE GREAT COMMISSION." (Matthew 28:18-20).

All who will enlist are promised the accompanying presence and power of Jesus to make it work. "...I am with you always..." Paul increasingly identifies with the gospel from calling it, "The gospel, to our gospel, to my gospel". The most important thing we can do every day is to be a Full Time Participant, Example, Promoter and Witness of the gospel. The gospel affords the greatest richness available to each of us!

PORNOGRAPHY IS BAD BECAUSE

Pornography is obscene literature, music and pictures depicting sexuality outside the definition by normal and decent standards. Those who argue about morality being a matter of opinion are probably not going to see the difference between right and wrong.

What makes pornography so evil is that sexuality is taken out of normal context and exaggerated as to its function, pleasure and purpose. It takes it out of a marriage setting and magnifies it out of proportion with the rest of life. It is especially tragic when presented to the young in such a warped way during their formative years. Many do not have the personal integrity, family support or religious conviction to help them look the other way.

Incest, unwanted pregnancies, disease and a host of other problems result from the attitudes and activities which follow. Bodies, glands and hormones are neither moral nor discreet by themselves; guided by a sense of right and wrong, the Bible and clean morality, sexuality is a wonderful and necessary gift of God. When constantly stimulated by music, literature, pictures and people exposing themselves, it can become an abusive beast, a transmitter of disease, a destroyer of happiness, health, family life and the soul.

Anger + D = Danger

I have seen a lot of people make fools of themselves in anger and in fact, one of those, I call "yo, moi, me". It has been said, "An angry man is again angry with himself when he returns to reason. Anyone can get angry, that is easy, but to be angry with the right person, to the right degree, at the right time, for the right purpose and in the right way—that is not within everybody's power and is not easy."

We tend to make up in wrath what we lack in reason; in anger we lose the realignment of cultured decency. ANGER IS ONE LETTER SHORT OF DANGER. A person fully angered is like a runaway train without an engineer, playing havoc with all in the way. We have devised "how to" techniques to cool us off or buy time, like "count to ten, hold your breath, etc" and with limited value. Anger is like a loaded and cocked pistol which we carry in our bosom; it could go off at any time and carrying it will ruin our health, our friendships and our chance of fulfillment.

The Bible admonishes, "Don't let the sun go down on your wrath and cease from anger." (John 15). But how? Christianity fully understood and experienced helps us to lay that gun down or better yet, never to pick it up! The Holy Spirit gives love, self-control, patience and more to those who ask! (Galatians 5:16-23). Vital Christianity is designed to give us "personal sovereignty"! (John, Chapter 15).

Advice to Those Living
On Residual Grace

Someone solicited my advice in trying to get "back on track," religiously. He had been uprooted from his familiar setting and had not been able to take root in a strange place. He was now carrying his religion, no longer being consciously carried by his faith. His patience was wearing thin, his love strained, his witness weak and his temptations were appealing. His discomfort was indeed the best thing he had going for him.

Religious matters are fundamental and when the foundation begins to crack, the whole house could soon crumble. Such is the plight of many who find themselves existing on residual grace (help) with no fresh re-supply, as a soldier cut off from the logistics re-supply systems of his army. Much of the inconsistency in our lives is due to "anchor slippage"; we stray away from our source of strength.

Likening Himself to a vine and us to branches, Jesus said, "Unless you abide in me and I in you, you will die." (John15:1-6). What distinguishes the "saints" among us from the general church crowd is they have learned how to stay in a constant receiving mode. The problem with my friend was not that God was giving him less but he was no longer in a receptive order. My advice to him? Become an active part of a Bible believing church, shore up your private and personal devotions of prayer and Bible reading, and take interest in others by witnessing, helping, and sharing your faith. (John 17:23).

New Year, Old Story

The children of Israel stood on the East bank of the river, their oppositions were overcome one by one until only the Jordan River was between them and their goal. They were instructed to, "Sanctify yourselves and follow the Ark of the Covenant, for you have not passed this way before..." (Joshua, Chapter 3). Following God's instructions, they crossed over into full access of the land God had given them.

As we enter the dawning of a new year, warring powers of Armageddon proportions stare at and threaten each other across the sand dunes of Biblical and historic lands. The name of our country and its people are among the objects of the greatest hate and their false god is said to be having great heavenly rewards for killing Americans. We must check the baggage of our spirit, soul and body and, with God's help, lay aside everything which could hinder our life in the new year. We must leave behind all hurt feelings, impure ambitions, prejudices and all attitudes which are contrary to our Father's will.

Let us fill our lives with good and proper things. The Christ of Christmas calls out to all, saying, "Wear My Yoke- for it fits perfectly and let me teach you..." All who will yoke up with Jesus will succeed with living. (Matthew 11:28-30). The Greatest Poverty is to be without His Salvation—The Greatest Wealth is to have His Salvation! He is Knocking at your Heart's Door—LET HIM IN NOW!!! (Romans 10:6-13).

THE SERMON ON THE MOUNT

God's true religion is pure and relevant at its origin; it is at our level that it can degenerate and deteriorate. Here, religious teaching and practice often become irrelevant and even cruel. Probably more offense, hurt and bloodshed have resulted around religious fervency than any other cause. What is a constant and stable church kingdom, for many of us, is a place where we slip, slide and stumble.

It seems that every generation needs to have a revival of renewal or "Sermon on the Mount" to recapture the spirit, expand the grasp and realign doctrine. The kingdom is not lacking for power to those whose values and concentration is there. In the "Sermon on the Mount," Jesus resets the tone of true religion. There, the whole of human religiosity is examined, compared and refocused.

It is in our interest to see it God's way because "He is the Way, the Truth and the Light." Those who want to make true religion bend for them are like the drowning man who wants to dictate the terms by which he will accept his rescue. (Matthew, Chapters 5-7).

THE RENT VEIL

A seldom mentioned, yet most significant fact is the rending of the veil in the temple when Jesus died. In Old Testament days, once a year, the High Priest appealed to God in the Most Holy Place for the needs of the people. A thick curtain separated the people from where God's presence was and access was by mediation only.

At the moment of Jesus' death, the veil was torn from top to bottom, signifying a new and continual access to God for all the people. The rend from top to bottom suggests God's initiative in removing all obstacles for an easy and confident approach to each other. We no longer need to wait for an appointed time or for an appointed person to approach God for us. He has decreed an open door policy for us all; a door which no man can shut.

We may now boldly and personally speak with Him, Sabbath or weekdays, day or night, in and out of church. The ground work has been carefully laid through many centuries for this day of greater access to Deity. We are only beginning to grasp the "deeper Spirit life" made available to those who will move toward the rent veil. (Mark 15:37-39).

THE REACH OF GOD

If God's reach was not longer than ours, we would all be lost. God, who at sundry times and in diverse manners spoke, "…hath in these last days spoken to us by His Son." The Bible records a progressive reach of God toward us. Each step exceeds the previous one in His continuing attempt to rescue and remedy a lost creation. Had we not been created with an ability to choose, He could easily move us in the right direction, like moving checkers on a board, but our existence would not have meaning.

The Old Testament gave us rules to live by, exposing our weakness so we could see that the nature of our problems demands help from Him. In our estranged state we are vulnerable, doing all kinds of crazy things called sin. In the New Testament approach, the most recent of God's progressive outreach, "we are drawn close to Him by a new and living way." (Hebrews 10:19-23).

Our basic problem is separation from our life source; to be saved is to be brought back into God's productive closeness where we are happy, strong and fulfilled. In Christmas we celebrate His arrival; in Good Friday, His paying our sin debt; in Easter, His resurrection to intercede for us; and in Pentecost, the Holy Spirit to empower us. There is much more to occur!

THE MAKING OF SAINTS

God's salvation is redemptive and also remedial. IF WE RECEIVE ONLY HIS PARDON OF OUR SINS THEN WE HAVE LOST OUR GUILT, BUT KEPT OUR WEAKNESS. Imputed righteousness, the goodness of Christ credited to us, has Biblical basis; but our salvation is also designed to save us from our sinful ways.

The emphasis we must be hearing from the church is that the grace of God has come to save us from the past and for the future. God is in the business of developing saints from people just like us, who live and work in this present world. Their lives are brought into harmony with His, loving and feeling as He does about the issues at hand. Gaining the approval of God of the way we live is the highest credential on earth! The deeper we relate with God, the more deeply we will openly relate with our fellow humans and their problems.

May God make His own declaration of who are His saints, but let us highlight those among us who are developing into the salvation state called "saved to the uttermost." (Hebrews 7:25). A shortage of good examples has become a national crisis with far reaching consequences. (Romans 1:7-8).

OUR FATHER WANTS US TO SUCCEED

Our usual gift to high school and college graduates is to frame their invitation or certificate and with admonition written on the back: "Congratulations! Live by these three rules and you will be successful: First, obey God. Second, respect all people. Third, apply your abilities vigorously." They and their families are appreciative that the whole secret to successful living can be grasped so concisely.

There will be occasions when there will be strong temptations to break out of the guidelines; we think we cannot afford to tell the truth, or respect others, or work hard, but we must persevere. So-called success, attained in rebellion against our Creator's laws and at disadvantage to our fellow humans, is false success; it is actually failure measured by a false standard. Success will not be measured by what we garner into our sphere of possessions, but by our contributions, or input into other lives, and by our motives.

In the end we will be judged by Him who knows the whole truth about us. We will have failed, if He is not pleased by the way we have lived. Join me, please, this day in purposing to live by these simple rules in the yet unspoiled year. Our Father is looking for people with high and noble goals: He wants to help us succeed. (Psalm, Chapter 73).

SEX EDUCATION

We've heard it said, "Sex—the Victorians pretended it didn't exist, the moderns pretend that nothing else exists." The difference between male and female and the attraction which that difference generates is God's design. The corruption and elevation of sexuality out of context to the whole life experience is our doing.

Human sexuality carries the potential for great happiness and also for extreme misery. If the "love of money is the root of all evil," uncontrolled sex must be the nearest runner up. Probably the greatest human challenge is our responsibility to manage and regulate our own sexual behavior. The bad which ensues must be credited to our choosing to violate moral principles.

Our great American problem is the over glorification of sex and elevating it out of proper proportion to the whole normal life. Our all qualifying buzz word "sexy" has become the standard by which all things are measured, even human life. We do not need and indeed cannot sustain all the attention and encouragement given to sex.

The fear of sex education which is not taught in a context or moral considerations is a reasonable and legitimate fear. Mismanaged sexuality has the power to mess up our life on earth and keep us out of heaven.

More than Conquerors

Our Lord and His Bible have made no demands nor set goals for us which are unattainable. Within the provisions of the Holy Spirit are most of the answers to spiritual anemia and failure in individual and church life. While Christmas opens the door to the events of Good Friday and Easter, in Pentecost we celebrate the life of God coming to empower the believers.

So important was the Holy Spirit's coming that Jesus seemed eager to leave: "It is necessary that I go or the Spirit cannot come." This life of God is indispensable power for individuals and the church. It is that which maintains the large difference between worldly institutions and the kingdom of God on earth. Christ's last words were instructions to prepare to receive His Spirit. (Acts1:4-8).

If an individual or a church will ask for this power and continue in a receptive mode, they will not be denied. (Luke 11:13). A lot of human foolishness and error may abound in the name of the Holy Spirit, but those who sincerely seek to live in this grace and power of God will live in all-Christian adequacy and competence. (Romans, Chapter 8; John, Chapter 14).

LIFE IN BALANCE

I overheard someone say, "I wish I could tell you how wonderful it is to be well-rounded." Obviously, that person had been the victim of a disproportionate lifestyle and had somehow come to have his life brought into balance. Bringing our lives into right proportions is an important goal in the Christian message.

The Bible cautions against overeating, love of money, substance abuse, worry, selfish attitudes, and more. Yes, it even says, "Don't be too religious." (Ecclesiastes 7:16). Sexuality is promoted far beyond the Creator's intent, and the excesses are playing havoc with homes, little children, and the abusers themselves. Deficiencies here and excesses there lessen the quality of life and create problems for us and those we love.

Managing one's life is the most important assignment a person will ever be given, and if one fails there, he will fail everywhere. Our personal disorders will carry over to our work and friendships, undermining and destroying all. Some lives are just beginning to lose balance; others have gone the whole distance of depravity's fall. To all of us who suffer, Christ offers BALANCE. (John 10:10). He gives us the ability to control our lives.

HIGH NEED, LOW COMMITMENT

A great Chinese leader once said that what amazed him about the American Christians is that, "They always talk about how much they can ask of God and so seldom of how much God is able to ask of them." Someone else described our present attitude as being "high in need and low in commitment."

Those who have not noticed the abundance of God's demands and expectations have done a lot of skipping over and around in their Bible reading. He expects discipline and deep involvement with Him in His worthy goals: "And so, dear brothers, I plead with you to give your bodies to God. When you think of what He has done for you, is this too much to ask?" (Romans 12:1). The unfinished work of Christ is the application of those benefits which He paid for on the cross.

Each of us is a link between God and someone who may have no other chance to know the love of God! The most important thing we will ever do is to share the love of God always everywhere and in every way possible. (Matthew 28:18-20). "We are laborers together with God..." (1 Corinthians 3:9).

ADAM'S APPLE

The Genesis account of Adam's eating the forbidden fruit is the Bible's way of telling us that we had a good thing going, but our first parents goofed off our inheritance. Beyond all doubts, that initial departure from God's protective will is the worst thing which ever happened. The origin of evil on earth can be traced back to that first disobedience in Eden.

Since then, we have been developing our humanistic attitudes and approaches to Life. No human activities or learning are without obvious marks of our fallen state. Evil thrives among us when we shut ourselves from God's protective rules. Everyday, the news carries sad accounts of some of us who have gone the full distance of depravity's fall. How stupid, how brutal, how vicious, and how selfish we can become in our estrangement from God. We aren't being punished for Adam's sin, but we are disadvantaged by being born and nurtured in a sinful environment.

Christ's mission to earth was to give us all a chance to start anew with God. He has instructed His church to go to all peoples and to make clear expression of invitation for Him (John 3:16; Matthew 28:18-20).

ACCOUNTABILITY

The word <u>accountability</u> is now frequently showing up in church-related talk or writings. Scandal in the church is not new, nor is greed in the Holy Place. The difference is that Judas accepted 30 pieces of silver for selling his Lord, while recent sellouts of the church's reputation and honor are tallied in millions of dollars.

None rejoice more than the faithful Christians when they see the house of God being cleansed of selfish "money changers." They know that unscrupulous and unholy attitudes in "God's building" are far more disastrous than revealing embarrassments on the outside. Only those with the poorest of judgment would quit the church because Judas, the first Christian treasurer, was a thief or that poor depraved humanity can produce occasional defilers of sacred trust.

Let's not forget that the work of God must have money to operate and that God's system of the "tithe and offerings" is a good, reasonable, and fair way to finance the most important institution on earth. Yes, the word accountability should have a place up there by the more Biblical words, such as saved, holy, love, honor, heaven.

One for the "Critters"

When I was a child, there was a saying that, on New Year's Eve at exactly midnight, animals could talk. I suppose it is true that animals talk (not only once a year and, of course, only in animal language.) What advice, complaints, or pleas might they wish to register with us if, occasionally, we could communicate? The hunted might want equal opportunities, the caged would tell us how awful it is to lose one's freedom, and the domesticated might tell how hard it is to live and be kicked around in a people's world.

God gave man charge of the earth with all its life. He was to name them, respect their needs, and be kind of a god to them, a merciful and considerate protector. Could this earth function without animal life? They are all very important to the delicate balance of nature. We litter their grounds, poison their waters, encroach on their territories, pollute their air, and kill them for the fun of it. They have neither money nor means to hire lobbyist, elect representatives or organize resistance. Failure in environmental responsibilities is to fail the very first assignment God gave us. In failing our Creator, we are failing ourselves. We need a revival of awareness of our environment and all of its life. (Genesis 1:1-31).

ALL ABOUT A CONNECTION

True religion is about a connection between God and man in which God clears our record and replaces our bad and weakness with His good and strength; it is designed to carry us rather than our carrying it. Jesus said that the religion He brought down from heaven works on the same principle as a vine-branch relationship, that as a branch bears the natural qualities of its parent plant, we would naturally and easily experience and exhibit godly qualities. (John, Chapter 15).

Our responsibility is to stay connected to our life source. All individual and church activities are of value to the extent that they enhance and reinforce that relationship. It is the continual and immediate flow from vine to branch which gives life and produces fruit. True religion is about the life of God coming to us; Paul said, "I live, yet not I, Christ lives in me."

In Adam, we developed a connection problem; Jesus came to reconnect us to our life source. Becoming saved and the Christian life is all about a connection! Jesus said, "Come unto me, all you who labour and are heavy laden and I will give you rest..." (Romans 10:6-13; Acts 2:38-39; Galatians 5:16).

One Red Rose

A dear friend died, and a beautiful red rose lay across her chest. The family had been asked by an appreciative caller if it would be all right to place this rose in her hand. The story is that the caller was once in deep personal trouble, and our friend had patiently helped her get on a winning course. Had we all so thoughtfully responded, the casket would have been full of roses.

The world is full of people who see others through opportunistic eyes, stepping stones on their way to prideful and selfish living. Our world affords us too few good examples of what life is all about. Too many of our heroes inspire us to be selfish, and we live our lives with little or no regard for others—at worst we hurt, at best we ignore them.

Our Creator's goal is to develop us into observant, compassionate and helpful human beings. All of us should understand that our blessings are intended to be shared, or else we are not worthy of our trust. There is something vulgar about need and plenty, wholeness and want, joy and sadness living side by side. Does God care about the suffering, the deprived and the hurting? He does and has equipped us to help Him bring their answer! We are at our very best when we can be touched by the hurting of others.

P.S. "Thanks, Vera Ellis, enjoy your rest!"

WHATEVER HAPPENED TO SIN?

Nobody wants to be called a sinner anymore; we've conjured up more tame words which free us from responsibility for our conduct. The guilty is "temporarily insane," the drunk is "diseased," antisocial behavior is "environment related" and sexual irresponsibility is "well it just happened."

It is a new twist on the old Biblical word "hypocrite"; we don't deny the act, we deny responsibility for it. We are becoming a spoiled people whose five senses have become gods which demand fresh sacrifices day and night. To many, the Ten Commandments are no more than "ten suggestions" which are far too idealistic for modern man. Fewer voices are warning us that "the wages of sin is death..." When we contemplate Christ's remedial measures, we can understand the seriousness of our sin problem.

We need to take positive moral positions and point out that "right is strong and smart, while wrong is weak and stupid." Let us not resent but thank those who point out our sin. Sin is a vicious killer of all which is good and important to us; Christ came to free us from its grip on our lives. (John 3:16-17; Romans 10:2-13; Acts 2:37,40).

GOD'S ORDER

I was in a very different kind of church service recently, one of those about which some members say, "Thank God, the preacher didn't get to preach!" The pastor is a good speaker, but he seemed to not have clear direction. The service took on a Quaker-like spontaneity while various ones stood and forcefully contributed a mini-message or song or scripture. Someone learned over and whispered, "This is body ministry." Well, different it was, and we all felt good about it—we all knew that we had heard from God and that was the way He wanted it this time.

Could it be that we are worshipping God in a manner we feel He deserves and is proper for deity, yet He longs for adoration from the heart? We give Him "formal order" and He may sometimes prefer "emotional freshness." We invite the Holy Spirit to take charge but leave Him little maneuverability around our rigid schedule. Yes, we owe God and the congregation order and preparedness and also room for the Holy Spirit to work.

I believe that Christ still reviews His churches (Revelations, Chapters 1-3) and sometimes says, "...I will come unto thee quickly, and will remove thy candlestick out of his place, except thou repent." If God's order prevails, we will always have wholesome and enriching variety!

Is This Your Final Answer?

The now popular question "Is this your . . . final answer?" is being asked in mom's kitchen, at play, at work and I have heard it in church. The *"Who Wants To Be a Millionaire"* show padded its producer's ratings and bank account and has turned "tired couch potatoes" into loud sweating quarterbacks. Some contestants walk away with large checks and others leave looking like they could crawl into the nearest, darkest hole they can find—their final answer was wrong.

Intelligent, involved humans as far back as Adam and Eve have had to make unavoidable, tough decisions. Few, if any, are without regret that a final answer had not been tempered with more knowledge, experience, patience, love or tolerance. The person who, with God's help, has settled for what is right and against wrong will succeed with living! It is a negotiable conscience which will get us into trouble.

When the matter of right and wrong is settled in our heart, the "final answer" is here, ready to be voiced without hesitation. Have you given Jesus your final answer? There are no disadvantages in saying yes! There is much more to gain or lose than $1,000,000. (Romans 10:6-13).

LAW AND GRACE

There always was confusion about Law and Grace. That is, Old Testament and New Testament religious practices. The Christianized Jews could not understand how practices promoted and cherished could now be of no importance. Much of the New Testament was written to settle this. Why? Did God change His mind? Did He not do it right at first?

No, God's plan is progressive—one stage prepares us for another; law prepared us for grace and grace prepares us for heaven. Ceremonial law is fulfilled in the passion of Christ and the experience of the church. The moral content, expressed by the Ten Commandments, is written on the consciences of those living in Christ.

A renewed mind and conscience is more sensitive than written rules. For example, the conscience would carry "Thou shalt not kill" to include reputation, good name, happiness and opportunities. Many continue to live by the limited checks and balances of written rules. They, like Old Testament believers, are legalistic and their morality is rigid while the spirit of the law is often strained or broken. Christ's goal is to bring us into extreme sensitivity about right and wrong by the continual in-dwelling Holy Spirit. He wants to write His laws in detail, "not on tables of stone but on tablets of human hearts." (1 Corinthians 3:3).

Our Father Wants Us to Be Friendly

The poorest people are those who have no friends. We are social creatures and friendship is high on the list of human needs; our humanness requires us to relate to others with friendliness.

Friendship is the strongest of voluntary relationships; it is affordable by all and no contribution is so important. Mature friendship is not selective but is like a stream of fresh water which is available for all who thirst. It does not exploit and is not ashamed of associations. True friendship corrects gently, it speaks truth measured out in kind language, and covers shame while it announces honor. It sets all at ease in its presence, favors granted are forgotten and love received is remembered. Openness and transparency (truth living) are hallmarks of mature friendship.

Our Creator's goal is that we become transmitters of friendly signals in all directions. Friendship should permeate all services, sales, and other human functions. It should exude on our streets, crowded restaurants and tension-filled offices, as well as in church functions. Christ said to His followers, "…I call you friends…" He knew that friendship, like a full fountain, would quench every human thirst. (John 15:15).

POWER FAILURE

Many years ago, Bro. George Baggett, the Sunday School Superintendent of our little church, asked every person to commit Galatians 5:22-23 to memory, "...The fruit of the Spirit is love, joy, peace, long-suffering, gentleness, goodness, faith, meekness, self-control..." The following Sunday, we were all called to recite these two verses. He was an established Christian who knew that we had to understand the source of Christian life and power or we would fail at living.

Our lives are spent "hoping and working" hard toward achieving the contents of these verses. They are the things of which the good life is made but most look for them in all the wrong places. World religions and secular philosophies promote these ideals. They develop formulas of meditation and discipline to achieve peace, joy, self-control.

The Holy Spirit gives these qualities in their purest form to those who ask! The way of victorious and joyous Christian living lies in the continual and immediate work of the Holy Spirit in the soul which clings to Christ. We can attribute most "Christian Power Failure" to our lack of serious appreciation for the Holy Spirit. (Luke 11:11-13).

Science and Religion

Science and religion are of the same parentage and are like Jacob and Esau who fought in their mother's womb. God, wanting to divulge His mysteries, employs science to study nature's secrets and religion to make known His morality and intentions for His Creation.

In identifying Nature's work, we are freed to see Deity apart from the powers of Nature. These two agencies of God need to move from adversarial attitudes to appreciation and cooperation. Both are victims of overdeveloped traditions, incapable of self-evaluation. They severely penalize those who break out of their crusty old mental molds and needed change is too slow.

Science seeks truth yet bogged down with an atheistic mind-set, keeps digging old graves to support its inbred views of creation without God. Religion is too divided over minor differences, sets perimeters and severely punishes those who dare challenge the established order. They both need to get over knee-jerk responses to each other's blunders and vocabulary and face to face, ask questions of each other. I have a feeling they both have much more to discover and report!

Sun, Stand Still

I heard an otherwise intelligent man discredit the whole Bible because Joshua commanded the sun to stand still at the battle of Jericho, rather than the earth to hold on rotation. Who, I wonder, speaks with all scientific correctness among us; surely we'd run him out of town. We all know better and we still say, "The sun rises and sets."

It is very foolish for us to be disappointed because the Bible is honest and records the falterings and ignorance of people while they are learning to walk with God. If we read the Bible properly, we will discover He is trying to teach us to walk upon a highway of holiness. Most importantly, we will see the love of God beckon us from every page to accept His help. The Bible, a journal of God and man's relationship, tells us where we have been, where we are, and where we are going.

Let those who believe they see error read it again; and, if they still believe they see fault, let them charge it to the depravity and ignorance of man. Better yet, let them blame their own inability to grasp its intended message. The Bible does not claim that all whose names appear in it grasped all scientific truths, nor that her writers attained perfection. (1 Corinthians 13:9-10). She has decreed that all who read her with love and sincerity will learn her mysteries.

THE ORDINARY THINGS

Normal living is made up of long stretches of very ordinary activities with an occasional "super happening." It is in the conducting of those common activities that success or failure results. Days, months and years of hard, dull labor precede all accomplishments, whether receiving an award, signing a document or dedicating a building.

Christianity has very little record of fantastic happenings. Very few have walked on water, seen angels or been to heaven and back; most have not had "earthshaking experiences," yet we are secure in our faith. Those who must have the spectacular will soon be disappointed because God distributes those in limited measure, but His power is always at work in the ordinary chores of life.

The Bible urges us to "fight the good fight", "endure hardness" and "walk by faith" when the feelings aren't there. God's specialty is the transforming of defeated and mismanaged lives into wholesome order. All who will open the ordinary affairs of their lives to God's "Son Shine" will see clearly and will succeed with living! (Romans 12:1-2).

MY GENERATION IS FAST SLIPPING AWAY

My generation was born in the late twenties and early thirties, in the grip of the Great Depression. Living simply, close to the soil and nature, they were neighborly, loyal, and patriotic. They participated in the advent of rural electrification, television, the industrial and technological revolutions. They lived by three rules in this order: fear and respect God, don't soil the family name, and earn your way in life.

In our neighborhood, the strongest drugs available were "Cajun dark coffee and Black Diamond Tobacco." The unmarried's interest in sex was limited to curious talk, and youthful differences were settled not with guns but with bare fists. Their morality was cast in conservative Christianity and the word "errancy" never referred to the Bible. They fought in two wars of liberation and set out to remove the last traces of racial discrimination. Young people were taught to respect their elders and what the preacher, priest, doctor, policeman, and school teacher said was "gospel".

Now, many are worried about their children's future, about their churches, country, national disasters like 911 and more. Yes, they also have sins to repent of but they are unique in that their lives straddle the old ways and the new. Many plowed with their dad's mules and oxen or washed with their mom's scrub board, and now have their own PC. They feel qualified to judge. Obituary columns are listing them daily by the dozens. With their passing also go precious values which we cannot afford to lose.

The Peacemakers Shall Be Called "The Children of God"

We are social creatures; that is we are created with a need to belong, to be loved, protected and helped by others. This ranks high—after our need for God; perhaps just under our need for air, water, and food. This social need calls for giving, as well as receiving; it is a built-in trade off with every sensitive guideline.

This commonwealth access is a vast reservoir of knowledge and security systems which we cannot do without. When we are down, it picks us up and when we are too high, it cuts us down. Some give up on their kind; they have an unrealistic view of how things ought to be; others are ill equipped to handle the frequent breakdowns in interrelationships. They are too sensitive about their own hurt and are unaware of how they may hurt others. The price we must pay for the privilege of living together is that we sometimes hurt each other. Those who drop out pay a much greater price; they sacrifice helping and being helped.

No one is so completely endowed that he or she needs no one. God said, "It is not good that man should be alone." By creating Adam and later Eve, God envisioned family, neighbors, workers, church groups, and nations of people helping each other. (Genesis 2:18). Jesus said, "Blessed are the peacemakers for they shall be called the children of God." When we are at peace and help others live in peace, we are in the most secure, giving, and receiving position with God and each other. OUR FATHER IS IN SHORT SUPPLY OF PEACEMAKERS; would you help Him, help us? "For we are labourers together with God..." (I Corinthians 3:9; Ephesians, Chapter 2).

Let Her Alone, She Has Done What She Could

Jesus and friends were in the house of Simon the leper, eating a meal and a woman having an alabaster box of very expensive ointment slipped in, broke the box and poured the contents on Jesus' head. We can't help but wonder how and where she broke the box and how this affected Jesus' lunch. Immediate criticism of her action followed with the words: "murmured, indignation, waste, and probably what a mess."

Jesus said, "Let her alone; why trouble ye her; she hath wrought a good work on me . . . she hath done what she could; she is come a forehand to anoint my body to the burying. Verily I say unto you, wherever this gospel shall be preached throughout the whole world, this also that she hath done shall be spoken of for a memorial of her."

She had one window of opportunity to honor Him and she did it; caring only what pleased Him. I am compelled to press you and me: Have we; are we doing what we can to honor Christ, to comfort the grieving, to bring the Spirit of Christ into the situation we are now facing which is critical to people's salvation, fulfilling life, and survival? Are we living in such dedication, attitude and example that our life is like a Bible to those who are lost? Could Jesus say about us; not once in a while but every day, "HE AND SHE ARE DOING ALL THEY CAN, EVERY MINUTE, HOUR, DAY, WEEK, MONTH, YEAR, OF THEIR LIVES." Let's Try!
(Mark, Chapter 14).

THE GREATEST INVITATION

"Come unto me, all ye that labor and are heavy laden, and I will give you rest. Take my yoke upon you and learn of me; for I am meek and lowly in heart and ye shall find rest unto your souls." (Matthew 11:28-29). Realizing our limitations, mortals should be careful to not over promise. Our commitments must be tempered with such words as, "If the Lord will."

However, Jesus could extend the above invitation without reservations. The notice is to ALL—the sinful, mean, the disgusting and the good to whom life is hard and burdens are heavy to carry. He said, "Come to me and I will give you rest." Religious invitations which ask less than coming to Jesus will not produce the "REST" or relief which the weary soul needs. Any invitation which offers less than a personal contact with the Christ of Christianity will fall short of supplying all the human needs.

He invites us to yoke ourselves with Him; our problems lie in our wrong connections and our trying to live without His help. The Christ, by whose power the worlds were made and held in order, invites us to connect with Him; order and rest will follow!

RELIGION OF THE HEART

I have seen a lot of people who know very little about Christian theology and have a poor grasp of proper terminology, but really know God by experience. Paul speaks of their assurance, "The Spirit itself beareth witness with our spirit, that we are the children of God." (Romans 8:16).

They are like the thief on the cross who said, "Remember me when you come into your kingdom." Everybody knows he should have made his public profession more in keeping with standardized language as, "I accept Christ as my personal Savior," or other church recognized formulas. He didn't use the right words but seems to have gotten more than he asked for.

There can be a lot wrong with our mental grasp, but if the spiritual heart is open to God, all necessary benefits will follow. It is at that moment that "the prodigal has come home." Now having been forgiven, the life of God begins to sanctify and remedy every area of the fallen soul. In time, the head and language will catch up with the experience of the heart. The nature of our lostness is that we are far from our Father. By the door which Jesus opened, we trust unto salvation, a salvation with unending benefits! (Romans 10:6-12).

THE GREATEST CALL

"Answering the call" is a common Christian term to speak of our positive response to something which needs to be done in the church. Many testify of specific and personal experiences which let them know exactly what they are to do, while others volunteer in response to obvious needs.

The Bible speaks of five ministries and Spiritual gifts which bring maturity, knowledge, wisdom and power to the New Testament Church, making it the most responsive and strongest institution on earth. (Ephesians 4; 1 Corinthians, Chapter 12). All these services must function with and in God's love or they will distract rather than enhance the work of Christ.

Having said this, the Bible points out that the most permanent and practical call of God is for all of us to show Christian love continually and in every situation. When the work of the church on earth will end, these special ministries will end, but love, the love of God expressed through His people, will continue throughout eternity. Conducting our every human contact and enterprise in an atmosphere of God's love is the greatest call; the most effective and the most permanent. This must be our specialty and our commitment! (1 Corinthians, Chapter 13).

There Are Prisons without Bars

It is sad to see people whose conduct has led them to be locked behind prison bars. There are millions there who tried to bend advantage; their judgment failed and, again, justice prevailed. Millions more are free to roam but they are no less confined than those behind bars, guarded day and night.

There are many ways to get locked up; by drugs and drink, by anger, fear and stress, by mistrust and conscience full of guilt. Others are imprisoned by drab work outside their line of skill and more by problems wrought in thinking they don't need God nor their friends to help them out. Some are in chains of religious form; they find a thousand ways to make their religion leave them limp and weak. Others are driven by passions of greed and lust, whose five senses have become their gods who demand fresh sacrifices day and night. The victims of such depraving woes are reduced to barren lifeless form. They are like the waters of an ocean wave which beat against bold rocks on lonely beaches. They hesitate; they proceed and then fall back, never to surface again.

To all those cuffed and destroyed in spirit and soul, I point to the mighty Christ who stood affront of Lazarus' decomposing form. Against all objections, He said, "Proceed with the opening of the tomb!" Then with voice defiant and strong, He cried out, "COME FORTH, CUT HIM LOOSE, LET HIM GO!" Thus, did Christ set free one four days dead to prove that there is no lost cause, no sinful chains nor emotional bars too strong and if asked, He will SMASH TO BITS AND SAY, "LOOSE THEM AND LET THEM GO!" (John, Chapter 11).

THY WILL BE DONE

The greatest privilege on earth is to be able to call God, who created heaven and earth, Our Father. This privilege includes an invitation to prayer and His promises of answers. We are at our very best when we take a position in prayer; there is no time so well spent as time spent in prayer.

When we don't pray, we are actually saying in deed, "I don't need you Father; I can handle it by myself." "...Oh, what needless pain we bear all because we do not carry everything to God in prayer..." In His model prayer, Jesus instructed His disciples to say, "...Thy kingdom come, Thy will be done..." We should feel safe in requesting an answer to any situation which is in harmony with God's way of doing things. All our praying must reflect a desire for God's will and answers based on heavenly principles.

We should constantly review our position on all matters of life to be sure they are all "in His will." If we have to leave the will of God to be happy or prosperous or popular, that gain will soon turn into the bitterness of gall without God's support. (Matthew 6: 7-13).

Build Your House upon the Rock

It is much easier to build one's house on the sand than upon solid rock. No blistered hands on pick and shovel, no blasting is required. There are no long trenches to dig and fill with cement and steel. No long delays prevent our occupancy, no boring plans, no tests are required.

Too many hurriedly stack twigs on top of each other and call this home. Others pounce upon a course of life without time to educate and pray. They want to build too fast, before the mortar has time to dry and set. Some despise caution and virtue; life is a fun game without rules, they play.

In these competitive times we will need no less than excellence to survive. As in all in nature, only the most fit will perpetuate his kind. The strong will eat the weak or force them out and pass them by. This law has no moral concern; it's just a part of nature's rhythm and rhyme.

As sure as night follows day, your deeds will be put to test. There is a law which proves true in all lives, careers, and loves bequeathed. The winds of adversity will seek you out and put your strength to test.

It may be soon or years away, but howling fiery trials will reveal the weak. What is the rock upon which we must build and the substance we lay thereon? The rock is the TRUTH; truth about God, yourself, your world and all things made. Upon TRUTH, with dedication and care, lay all the ENERGIES of your triune life. Seek advice, weighed and measured, and be sure each stone is prayerfully laid.

The Grace of God in Me Stored

I pray for, yet I hope I shall never be so full, I need not struggle for my daily bread. I seek not to exterminate all that press against my goals. I resent neither those who disclose my wrongs nor the elements which drench my way. I dream neither for a life somewhere else removed nor for the advantages of another soul.

I will ask for and this I take; life as it is and I shall be victor, I shall not fail. I will walk among the thorns, I shall wrench bread by the sweat of my soul. I will not seek a path made smooth by other men, not walk the easy but the proper way. I shall press this life to yield its measure, no less than a hundred fold.

Man is wiser, stronger, faster and better when tested hard and fast. We are machines designed to function best in war than peace. We are never at our best without the howling winds of trouble and doubt. It is when we pit ourselves against a thousand odds that the adrenalin is released.

I like myself best when I am tried and proven true. But even when I've failed the test, I love to note the courage flow. Something in me says, "OK, you've failed but you must try again. Now then, fill bags with sand and stack them high so when the waves again invade you will withstand the foe."

I salute the grace which from God freshly flows. That grace which comes when faith and prayer together tap its source. But I have come to see grace much more, the grace of God which is in me stored.

THE COST AND JOY OF COMMITMENT

Commitment is an inner resolve and dedication to pursue a goal or to contribute to the accomplishment of a task. Commitment can have varying degrees of application of energy and resources. The range starts with sympathetic caring, and ends with total involvement of ourselves and our resources. No great accomplishments are made with less than total commitment. A project requires no less devotion than a mother's care for an infant. Goals are really the children of our souls which are totally dependent on our nurture and care in order to develop into maturity. Deep commitment, for good or evil, is the unavoidable ingredient which turns dreams into reality. Man, made in the image of God, with our modern means can truly move mountains.

A Christian will never know the extent of Holy Spirit power and wisdom waiting in reserve until he fully identifies with the Father's goals. (Acts 1:8). The "Lo I am with you to the end . . . ", applies to the involved in the process of outreach. (Matthew 28:18-20). The Holy Spirit given to equip us for service is a truth which many have not grasped. To them, involvement in the work of the kingdom of God means <u>cost</u>. In inactivity, we languish; in commitment we flourish because Holy Spirit energy is attracted to the activities of the kingdom.

Humanity reaches it's greatest distinction from all others of His creation when we are fully committed to take our place under God as executors of His goals. The cost incurred to us in sacrificial labor pales in view of the joyous dividends which accrue to the credit and the pleasure of the <u>totally committed</u>.

TWO BLIND MEN HELPED
ME TO SEE

I saw two blind men in Cordoba. They were walking arm in arm, flowing with the crowd and laughing loudly while they talked. They sorted out their way with canes which sensed their path ahead. I said to them, "Dear Sirs, I bid you stay for I have need to inquire of life, as you live; life so deprived of senses meant to be." "What is life without its sight? You who know no form, who cannot perceive what differs human flesh from that of beast and whose own features you cannot tell if they be comely or if they are fair." How can you tell what is meant for laughter and when do you know that you should cry? What is it that you can grasp of substance enough to laugh? Have you seen furry kittens play or little girls dressed in grown up's clothes?"

Said they, "Do you with eyes to see ask of the blind for light? If eyes are the only windows to the soul, then you should not inquire of blinded men. Come now our curious friend and join us in our walk. Close your eyes now clasp this pointed cane and go with us. Let nature's light shine through. Bare your soul and let it be bathed by her sounds and feels. Let God speak and His creation make room for you." They led me round from street to avenue, past streams and through the park. Said they, "We must move on, the threat of rain is in the air. Feel the air upon my face; it clings while moisture quickly moves to make drops heavy enough to rain. It must be Friday; the traffic is more alive on days of pay. Do you now smell the pollen of spring and out yonder to the right a mating pair of ducks I hear? Isn't it great to be alive?" they said, "And don't you grieve for those well endowed with windows to the soul who walk through these streets with blinders closed?"

I said, "Thank you sirs, I now see more. I shall no more sorrow only for those who use pointed sticks for eyes but I shall weep for all men though well endowed who live their lives with windows closed. Who think not, who with their spirit touch not God, who stumble through their entire lives blinded, unfeeling; lives lived completely without sight."

P.S. I saw these two men while on a mission in Cordoba, Argentina.

I Believe In God and I Have Decided To Be a Witness

I shall be a witness for God. I shall endeavor to give a witness on every occasion, in every place, in every circumstance and in all associations.

I shall not try to judge the bigness nor the smallness of the opportunity. My witness must be proper to the occasion; sometimes vocal, sometimes silent, but it shall carry a message in itself, a rebuke; a consolation or an exhortation for whatever the need might be.

I shall endeavor to make my witness a natural part of my life, like breathing; it must be something I don't consciously make happen or it will carry a hollow, annoying ring like sounding brass or tinkling symbols. I must witness out of a compassionate and generous heart; not as a necessity imposed on me. My awareness and compassion must develop and my witness must become part of my personality. I shall witness as I am given grace to witness. I shall seek guidance and power to witness. I must witness accurately and relative to the need. I shall endeavor to live my life at Spirit pitch, always learning more about God and man so that all advantages can come together in a vast reservoir of knowledge.

I shall not attempt to count success nor measure failure as I witness. I shall sow seed, water plants, cultivate and exploit opportunity. I must not witness more than can be received; I will be careful not to cram nor invade one's privacy.

I shall not wait to become perfect or I shall never witness, but I shall witness what I understand to be truth. I shall not forget that I too need help, so I shall be a student to all who can teach me. I shall witness what I was without Him, I shall witness what I am in Him; I shall witness what I shall be with Him.

I shall witness His peace in trouble. I shall witness His calm in turmoil. I shall witness His love for all in loving all. I shall witness His invitation into heavenly places by occupying my own place in Him.

I shall not say that this is a bad day or I dread tomorrow for I shall not resent what He lets happen in my life. I shall witness His sufficiency by being happy with my daily bread knowing that as each day will be, so will He measure out my blessings.

I shall witness in mistakes for I shall apologize. I shall witness in failure for I shall show courage. I shall witness in kindness, honesty, and fairness. I shall witness in success by being His faithful steward.

I shall witness God's decency by not laughing at dirty jokes. I shall witness His love by not retaliating. I shall witness His compassion by lending a helping hand. I shall witness His mercy by forgiving those who wrong me.

I shall witness at home, on the job, on the road, and in the stores. I shall witness in sunshine and rain, in profit and loss, in health or sickness. I shall witness before friends, family or strangers; by telephone, by letter, or in presence. I shall witness under the scourge of enemies and in the fellowship of believers. I shall witness in and out of season. I shall witness in power or weakness. I shall consider it noble to be His witness and I shall be conscious that the most important thing I will be, every day of my life, will be His witness.

We invite you to share your response to the
mini-messages in this book by writing to
Partners in Missions
P.O. Box 352,
Sulphur, Louisiana 70664
or Sidney Fontenot
1532 Ruby Lane,
Sulphur, Louisiana 70663
or to e-mail Sidney Fontenot at
parbonami@aol.com.

For additional copies you may order through
www.teamedupconsulting.com
or e-mail Debbie McCormick at
deb@debmccormick.com